Motivational Strategies in the Language Classroom

CAMBRIDGE LANGUAGE TEACHING LIBRARY

A series covering central issues in language teaching and learning, by authors who have expert knowledge in their field.

In this series:

Motivational Strategies in the Language Classroom

Zoltán Dörnyei

CAMBRIDGE
UNIVERSITY PRESS

CAMBRIDGE UNIVERSITY PRESS
Cambridge, New York, Melbourne, Madrid, Cape Town, Singapore, São Paulo

Cambridge University Press
The Edinburgh Building, Cambridge CB2 8RU, UK

www.cambridge.org
Information on this title: www.cambridge.org/9780521793773

First published 2001
7th printing 2007

Printed in the United Kingdom at the University Press, Cambridge

A catalogue record for this publication is available from the British Library

ISBN 978-0-521-79377-3 paperback

Contents

Contents

Acknowledgements

I am grateful to Cynthia Beresford, Péter Medgyes, Kálmán Németh, Mario Rinvolucri and Penny Ur, who first demonstrated to me what motivating language teaching was about in practice; the anonymous reviewers of the manuscript at its various stages, who have made some very constructive and insightful comments/suggestions; and Mickey Bonin from Cambridge University Press, who was there with advice and support right from the beginning when this book was only a vague idea.

Sincere thanks to you all and also to the many other people – family, friends, colleagues and students – from whom I have learnt about motivation during the past two decades.

Introduction: What this book is about and how it can be used

'Motivation is, without question, the most complex and challenging issue facing teachers today.'
(Scheidecker and Freeman 1999:116)

Long arguments can be put forward to prove that motivation is one of the key issues in language learning and that skills to motivate learners are crucial for language teachers, but you would not be reading this book if you were not aware of this. So, instead of doing the compulsory 'rounds' of highlighting the significance of motivation for teachers/students/researchers/educational policy-makers and practically everybody else, let me start this book by taking a very different approach.

Is there such a thing as 'motivation'?

Strictly speaking, *there is no such thing as 'motivation'*. Of course such a statement cannot stay in the introduction of a book on motivation without immediate qualification. What I mean is that 'motivation' is an abstract, hypothetical concept that we use to explain why people think and behave as they do. It is obvious that in this sense the term subsumes a whole range of motives – from financial incentives such as a raise in salary to idealistic beliefs such as the desire for freedom – that have very little in common except that they all influence behaviour. Thus, 'motivation' is best seen as a broad umbrella term that covers a variety of meanings.

Why do we use 'motivation' if its meaning is so vague? My guess is simply because it is a very convenient way of referring to what is a rather complex issue. For example, when we say that a certain student is 'motivated', most teachers and parents can well imagine what we mean – a keen, committed and enthusiastic learner who has good reasons for learning, who studies with vigour and intensity, and who demonstrates perseverance – yet it would be rather cumbersome to be more specific and list all these attributes. Similarly, we will have no problem envisaging an 'unmotivated' learner, even though, again, it might be quite tricky to describe exactly what this 'unmotivation' consists of.

The term is just as useful for theoreticians and researchers as for practitioners because it highlights one basic aspect of the human mind. This aspect is related to what one *wants/desires* (i.e. 'conative' functions), in contrast to characteristics related to what one *rationally thinks* (i.e. 'cognitive' functions) or *feels* (i.e. 'affective' functions). As Snow, Corno and Jackson (1996) summarise in the *Handbook of Educational Psychology*, this triadic distinction of the human mind (according to conation, cognition and affect) has been around for hundreds of years, and it is certainly a useful division when we consider specific learners: Aren't a student's 'keenness', 'cleverness' and 'temperament' obvious features to consider when we start describing someone in our class (e.g. *Rupert is a sensitive and bright student who is genuinely interested in history . . .*)?

To summarise, 'motivation' is related to one of the most basic aspects of the human mind, and most teachers and researchers would agree that it has a very important role in determining success or failure in any learning situation. My personal experience is that 99 per cent of language learners who really want to learn a foreign language (i.e. who are really motivated) will be able to master a reasonable working knowledge of it as a minimum, regardless of their language aptitude.

About the content of this book

This book is the first of its kind in the second/foreign language (L2) field that is entirely devoted to discussing *motivational strategies*, that is, methods and techniques to generate and maintain the learners' motivation. Although a great deal has been written in the past about *what* motivation is, describing its components and dimensions and how these influence learning, very little has been said about *how* this theoretical knowledge can be applied in the actual classroom. If classroom practitioners are thinking (justifiably) that researchers have generally left them to their own devices by not saying too much practically relevant about the topic, this book is intended to offer some remedy to that situation.

Although, as you will see, this is a practical book with only a limited theoretical discussion, the concrete classroom ideas that I will present are based on sound theoretical considerations. During the past two decades I have worked as a language teacher, teacher trainer, full-time researcher, university lecturer and PhD programme director, and the following chapters will contain the distillation of my own experiences, as well as a review of the relevant educational psychological and L2 literature. If you are interested in a more detailed discussion of the theoretical and research background of motivation, please refer to the 'Further reading' box at the beginning of Chapter 1.

How to use this book

As the author of this book, it may be surprising to hear me say that when I read books of the 'how-to-be-successful-in-business' or 'how-to-motivate-learners' type, they tend to make me feel inadequate and de-skilled rather than inspired. Even otherwise excellent manuals in educational psychology that are specifically designed for teachers can overpower with the wealth of ideas and recommendations they contain. During the process of writing this book, I became very much aware of the challenge of writing a 'what-to-do' book on motivation: How can we present a wide range of options for teachers to choose from that will inspire positive action? How can this presentation be rich and varied but avoid being daunting and making readers feel how complex the domain is and how much they are *not* doing?

In trying to respond to this challenge, I have tried to give the text three features that I feel are important, namely that it should be *short* (because few of us have much time in further education), *systematic* (because there is not much point in providing background material if it needs to be supplemented with other sources to get the full picture) and *interesting* (because I dislike boring books – although I admit that it is not that easy to write a 'pageturner' on motivation).

So what is the best way to use this book? The most obvious place to start reading any book is Chapter 1, but this may not be the best strategy in this case. Chapter 1 contains a theoretical overview of motivation which serves as background material and is not absolutely necessary for the successful adoption of motivational strategies. The classroom techniques are described in Chapters 2–5 and some readers may want to go there straight away. You may also decide to select a motivational area you are particularly interested in or concerned about from the table of contents or the subject index and look up the discussion of that particular issue, thereby using the text as a reference book.

A somewhat unorthodox approach might be – and this would be my recommendation to most readers – to start reading this book at the very end, that is, at the Conclusion. There I argue that in developing one's motivational repertoire it is not the quantity but the *quality* of the selected strategies that matters. Rather than trying to acquire all the strategies at once, for most people – certainly for me! – it is more useful to take a selective and stepwise approach, choosing a few strategies that would suit your teaching style and learner group well. In the light of this, the Conclusion offers general guidelines and concrete suggestions on how to achieve this gradual move towards a motivation-sensitive teaching practice.

All the best!

1   Background knowledge

Language teachers frequently use the term 'motivation' when they describe successful or unsuccessful learners. This reflects our intuitive – and in my view correct – belief that during the lengthy and often tedious process of mastering a foreign/second language (L2), the learner's enthusiasm, commitment and persistence are key determinants of success or failure. Indeed, in the vast majority of cases learners with sufficient motivation can achieve a working knowledge of an L2, regardless of their language aptitude or other cognitive characteristics. Without sufficient motivation, however, even the brightest learners are unlikely to persist long enough to attain any really useful language.

How true . . .

'The more teaching I observe (well over 500 lessons, by dozens of different teachers, over the last ten years, I recently calculated) the more strongly convinced I become that Motivation is What Matters – *if they gottit, ya laffin', if they don't, fergit it!'*
(From an e-mail message from Christopher Ryan, a teacher trainer friend)

In this chapter I would like to introduce the scene of motivation research both in educational psychology and in the L2 field. I will describe how various scholars have understood the notion of motivation in the past, what the contemporary trends are and how the theoretical knowledge can be turned into practical techniques to motivate language learners in the classroom. Last but not least, I will present a *taxonomy* of motivational strategies that will form the basis of the rest of the book.

Further reading

This book is intended to raise practical issues and make concrete suggestions for classroom practice rather than offer a comprehensive account of motivation theory. If you would like to know more about the theoretical background of the field, please refer to a recent summary, *Teaching and Researching Motivation* (Dörnyei 2001), which offers a comprehensive overview of the main issues and challenges in contemporary thinking about motivation. It also contains a detailed section on how to do research on motivation, providing guidelines for those who would like to conduct their own investigations. In addition, there is an up-to-date collection of 20 research studies that I have co-edited with Richard Schmidt from the University of Hawaii, *Motivation and Second Language Acquisition* (Dörnyei and Schmidt 2001), which contains contributions from international scholars from a wide range of motivational topics.

Within the field of educational psychology, I have found two books particularly useful: Jere Brophy's (1998) *Motivating Students to Learn* and Paul Pintrich and Dale Schunk's (1996) *Motivation in Education*. Concise and up-to-date summaries are also provided in the *Handbook of Child Psychology* (Damon and Eisenberg 1998) and the *Handbook of Educational Psychology* (Berliner and Calfee 1996).

1.1 Different approaches to understanding motivation

As discussed briefly in the Introduction, the term 'motivation' is a convenient way of talking about a concept which is generally seen as a very important human characteristic but which is also immensely complex. By using the term we can answer the question, *'Why does Rupert make such wonderful progress?'* by simply saying, *'Because he is motivated'*, without the need to go into details about what factors have contributed to this overall commitment. And just as conveniently, if Rupert is reluctant to do something, we can easily explain this by stating that *'He isn't motivated'* rather than having to elaborate on all the forces that have contributed to his negative attitude. In other words, 'motivation' is a general way of referring to the *antecedents* (i.e. the causes and origins) of action. The main question in motivational psychology is, therefore, what these antecedents are.

Because human behaviour has two basic dimensions – *direction* and *magnitude* (intensity) – motivation by definition concerns both of these. It is responsible for:

- the *choice* of a particular action;
- the *effort* expended on it and the *persistence* with it.

Therefore, motivation explains *why* people decide to do something, *how hard* they are going to pursue it and *how long* they are willing to sustain the activity.

All motivation theories in the past have been formed to answer these three questions but, quite frankly, none of them have succeeded fully. This is not very surprising, though: human behaviour is very complex, influenced by a great number of factors ranging from basic physical needs (such as hunger) through well-being needs (such as financial security) to higher level values and beliefs (such as the desire for freedom or one's faith in God). Can we blame motivational psychologists for not yet coming up with a comprehensive theory to explain the interrelationship of all these diverse motives?

Well said . . .

'Motivation, like the concept of gravity, is easier to describe (in terms of its outward, observable effects) than it is to define. Of course, this has not stopped people from trying it.'
(Martin Covington 1998:1)

You can probably imagine that when such a broad and important question as 'What causes behaviour?' is addressed, there is bound to be disagreement amongst scholars. Indeed, different schools of psychology offer very different explanations for why humans behave and think as they do, and there have been historical changes in our understanding of motivation, with different periods attaching importance to different aspects. In the first half of the twentieth century, the dominant views (such as Sigmund Freud's) conceptualised motivation as being determined by basic human *instincts* and *drives*, many of them being unconscious or repressed. Although such unconscious motives do not feature strongly in current motivational thinking, it seems clear that they play a significant role in our lives and therefore they are likely to be 'rediscovered' before long.

The middle of the twentieth century was dominated by *conditioning theories* related to behaviourist psychology, with a great deal of research focusing on how stimuli and responses interplay in forming *habits*. Although many of the findings were based on experiments with animals – such as Pavlov's dog or Skinner's rats – rather than humans, much of the acquired knowledge is still relevant for the understanding of issues like the role of practice and drilling, positive and negative reinforcement, or punishment and praise in learning.

The 1960s brought about further important changes. Partly as a counterreaction to the mechanistic views of behaviourism, humanistic psychologists such as Carl Rogers and Abraham Maslow proposed that the central motivating force in people's lives (unlike in rats' or dogs') is the *self-actualising tendency*, that is the desire to achieve personal growth and to develop fully the capacities and talents we have inherited. In his famous 'Hierarchy of Needs', Maslow (1970) distinguished between five basic classes of needs, which he defined as:

- *physiological needs* (e.g. hunger, thirst, sexual frustration);
- *safety needs* (need for security, order and protection from pain and fear);
- *love needs* (need for love, affection and social acceptance);
- *esteem needs* (need to gain competence, approval and recognition);
- *self-actualisation needs* (need to realise one's potential and capabilities, and gain understanding and insight).

These needs form a *hierarchy*, with the lower, physiologically based needs having to be satisfied first, before we can strive for the deeper happiness and fulfilment that comes from satisfying our higher-level needs.

The current spirit in motivational psychology (and in psychology in general) is characterised by yet another theoretical orientation, the *cognitive approach*, which places the focus on how the individual's conscious attitudes, thoughts, beliefs, and interpretation of events influence their behaviour; that is, how mental processes are transformed into action. In this view, the individual is a purposeful, goal-directed actor, who is in a constant mental balancing act to coordinate a range of personal desires and goals in the light of his/her perceived possibilities, that is his/her perceived competence and environmental support. In other words, whether people decide to do something is determined first by their beliefs about the values of the action, and then about their evaluation of whether they are up to the challenge and whether the support they are likely to get from the people and institutes around them is sufficient. It's all supposed to be very rational . . .

An overview of contemporary approaches in psychology

> ***Quite so!***
>
> 'With a hypothetical construct as broad and complex as motiva-
> tion, there is always room for controversy and argumentation.'
> (Raymond Wlodkowski 1986:12)

Within the overall cognitive view of motivation that characterises the
field today, we find a surprising number of alternative or competing
sub-theories. In order to understand the reasons for this diversity we
need to realise that the variety of motives that can potentially influence
human behaviour is staggering. Let us think for a moment of a range of
different reasons that, for example, could get a young woman, Jackie,
who is sitting on a bench in a park on a lovely afternoon, to stand up
and start running:

- She enjoys jogging.
- She has made a resolution that she will do some jogging every
  afternoon to improve her health.
- She would desperately like to lose some weight.
- Rupert appears jogging along the path and she wants to join him.
- Her athletics coach has just told her to get up and keep running.
- She is acting in a well-paid TV commercial advertising running shoes
  and the break is over.
- A black dog appears unexpectedly and starts chasing her.
- It has just started to rain.
- She realises that she has to fetch something from home quickly.

Obviously, the list is far from complete but it illustrates well that
motivation is indeed an umbrella-term involving a wide range of
different factors. This is why motivational psychologists have spent a
great deal of effort in the past trying to *reduce* the multitude of potential
determinants of human behaviour by identifying a relatively small
number of key variables that would explain a significant proportion of
the variance in people's action. In other words, the challenge has been
to identify a few central motives that are simply more important than
the others. Broadly speaking, different scholars have come up with
different 'most-important' motives, and this is what differentiates
between the various competing theories. Table 1 provides a summary of
the currently dominating motivational approaches.

Looking at Table 1, it must be admitted that each position in itself is

Table 1 *Summary of the most well-known contemporary motivation theories in psychology*

	GOOD SUMMARIES	MAIN MOTIVATIONAL COMPONENTS	MAIN MOTIVATIONAL TENETS AND PRINCIPLES
Expectancy-value theories	Brophy (1999), Eccles and Wigfield (1995)	Expectancy of success; the value attached to success on task	Motivation to perform various tasks is the product of two key factors the individual's *expectancy of success* in a given task and the *value* the individual attaches to success on that task. The greater the perceived likelihood of success and the greater the incentive value of the goal, the higher the degree of the individual's positive motivation (see also pp. 57–58).
Achievement motivation theory	Atkinson and Raynor (1974)	Expectancy of success; incentive values; need for achievement; fear of failure	Achievement motivation is determined by conflicting approach and avoidance tendencies. The positive influences are the *expectancy* (or perceived probability) of success, the incentive *value* of successful task fulfilment and *need for achievement*. The negative influences involve *fear of failure*, the incentive to *avoid* failure and the *probability* of failure.
Self-efficacy theory	Bandura (1997)	Perceived self-efficacy	*Self-efficacy* refers to people's judgement of their capabilities to carry out certain specific tasks, and, accordingly, their sense of efficacy will determine their choice of the activities attempted, the amount of effort exerted and the persistence displayed (see also pp. 86–87).
Attribution theory	Weiner (1992)	Attributions about past successes and failures	The individual's explanations (or 'causal attributions') of why past successes and failures have occurred have consequences on the person's motivation to initiate future action. In school contexts ability and effort have been identified as the most dominant perceived causes, and it is has been shown that past failure that is ascribed by the learner to low ability hinders future achievement behaviour more than failure that is ascribed to insufficient effort (see also pp. 118–122).

Self-worth theory	Covington (1998)	Perceived self-worth	People are highly motivated to behave in ways that enhance their sense of *personal value and worth*. When these perceptions are threatened, they struggle desperately to protect them, which results in a number of unique patterns of face-saving behaviours in school settings. (see also p. 88).
Goal setting theory	Locke and Latham (1990)	Goal properties: specificity, difficulty and commitment	Human action is caused by purpose, and for action to take place, *goals* have to be set and pursued by choice. Goals that are both specific and difficult (within reason) lead to the highest performance provided the individual shows goal commitment. (see also pp. 81–85).
Goal orientation theory	Ames (1992)	Mastery goals and performance goals	*Mastery goals* (focusing on learning the content) are superior to *performance goals* (focusing on demonstrating ability and getting good grades) in that they are associated with a preference for challenging work, an intrinsic interest in learning activities, and positive attitudes towards learning.
Self-determination theory	Deci and Ryan (1985), Vallerand (1997)	Intrinsic motivation and extrinsic motivation	*Intrinsic motivation* concerns behaviour performed for its own sake in order to experience pleasure and satisfaction such as the joy of doing a particular activity or satisfying one's curiosity. *Extrinsic motivation* involves performing a behaviour as a means to an end, that is, to receive some extrinsic reward (e.g. good grades) or to avoid punishment. Human motives can be placed on a continuum between self-determined (intrinsic) and controlled (extrinsic) forms of motivation.
Social motivation theory	Weiner (1994), Wentzel (1999)	Environmental influences	A great deal of human motivation stems from the sociocultural context rather than from the individual.
Theory of planned behaviour	Aizen (1988), Eagly and Chaiken (1993)	Attitudes; subjective norms; perceived behavioural control	*Attitudes* exert a directive influence on behaviour, because someone's attitude towards a target influences the overall pattern of the person's responses to the target. Their impact is modified by the person's *subjective norms* (perceived social pressures) and *perceived behavioural control* (perceived ease or difficulty of performing the behaviour).

very convincing: indeed, few people would find fault with the argument that people will only be motivated to do something if they expect success and they value the outcome (expectancy-value theories), or that it is the goal that gives meaning, direction and purpose to a particular action (goal theories). Neither would we question the fact that people are generally motivated to behave in ways that puts them in a better light (self-worth theory) or that if we lack confidence about being able to carry out a certain task, we are likely to avoid it (self-efficacy theory). It is also reasonable to assume that our past actions, and particularly the way we interpret our past successes and failures, determine our current and future behaviour (attribution theory), and that we will be more motivated to do something out of our own will than something that we are forced to do (self-determination theory). Finally, no one can deny that our personal likes and dislikes – i.e. attitudes – also play an important role in deciding what we will do and what we won't (theory of planned behaviour). In sum, all the different theories make a lot of sense; the only problem with them is that they largely ignore each other and very often do not even try to achieve a synthesis. This leaves us with a rather fragmented overall picture.

Well said . . .

'As a concept, motivation is a bit of a beast. A powerfully influential and wide-ranging area of study in psychology, motivation at its core deals with *why people behave as they do*. But in terms of mutual understanding and tightly controlled boundaries of application, motivation roams the field of psychology with almost reckless abandon. There are over twenty internationally recognised theories of motivation with many opposing points of view, differing experimental approaches, and continuing disagreement over proper terminology and problems of definition. . . . In the fields of instruction and learning this has led to some difficult problems – whom to believe, which theories to apply, and how to make sense out of this wealth of confusing possibilities. In general, instructors and trainers can find very few guidelines that suggest how to cohesively and consistently apply the most useful and practical elements from this extensive array of motivational information.'
(Raymond Wlodkowski 1986:44–45)

What kind of motivation theory do we need for practical purposes?

'Pure' theories of motivation, that is, models that represent a single theoretical perspective and are therefore anchored around a few selected motivational factors, while largely ignoring research that follows different lines, do not lend themselves to effective classroom application. Classrooms are rather intricate microcosms where students spend a great deal of their life. Besides being the venue where students acquire skills and learn about the world, classrooms are also where they make friends, fall in love, rebel against the previous generation, find out who they are and what the purpose of life is . . . in short, where they grow up. So much is going on in a classroom at the same time that no single motivational principle can possibly capture this complexity (cf. Stipek, 1996; Weiner, 1984). Therefore, in order to understand why students behave as they do, we need a detailed and most likely eclectic construct that represents multiple perspectives. Although some key motives do stand out in terms of their general impact on learning behaviours, there are many more motivational influences that are also fundamental in the sense that their absence can cancel or significantly weaken any other factors whereas their active presence can boost student achievement.

Well said . . .

'The real problem with motivation, of course, is that everyone is looking for a single and simple answer. Teachers search for that one pedagogy that, when exercised, will make all students want to do their homework, come in for after-school help, and score well on their tests and report cards. Unfortunately, and realistically, motivating students yesterday, today, and tomorrow will never be a singular or simplistic process.'
(David Scheidecker and William Freeman 1999:117)

An overview of approaches in the second language field

Traditionally, motivation research in the L2 field has shown different priorities from those characterising the mainstream psychological approaches. This has been largely due to the specific target of our field: *language*. It does not need much justification that language is more than merely a communication code whose grammar rules and vocabulary can be taught very much the same way as any other school subject. In a seminal paper written in 1979, the most influential L2 motivation researcher to date, Robert Gardner, argued forcefully that a second/foreign language in the school situation is not merely an 'educational phenomenon' or 'curriculum topic' but also a representative of the cultural heritage of the speakers of that language (Gardner, 1979). Therefore, teaching a language can be seen as imposing elements of another culture into the students' own 'lifespace'. In order to learn an L2, say French, students need to develop a French identity: they need to learn to think French and – though only partially and temporarily – also become a bit French.

True!

'Learning a foreign language always entails learning a second culture to some degree, even if you never actually set foot in the foreign country where the language is spoken. Language and culture are bound up with each other and interrelated. . . . People don't exist in a vacuum any more than club members exist without a club. They're part of some framework: a family, a community, a country, a set of traditions, a storehouse of knowledge, or a way of looking at the universe. In short, every person is part of a *culture*. And everyone uses a language to express that culture, to operate within that tradition, and to categorise the universe. So if you're planning to carry on some sort of communication with people who speak or write a given language, you need to understand the culture out of which the language emerges.'
(Douglas Brown, 1989:65)

The truth of the assumption that language and culture are inextricably bound together is clearly evidenced in situations where students for some reason do not like the L2 community and therefore refuse to incorporate elements of their culture into their own behavioural repertoire. For example, in Hungary, where I grew up, every school child was exposed to several years of learning Russian, the language of Hungary's communist Big Brother, with hardly any effect. As far as I am concerned, after studying Russian for over a decade, I cannot even recall its alphabet, which was normal at that time (and which I regret today).

Absolutely . . .

'There is no question that learning a foreign language is different to learning other subjects. This is mainly because of the social nature of such a venture. Language, after all, belongs to a person's whole social being: it is part of one's identity, and is used to convey this identity to other people. The learning of a foreign language involves far more than simply learning skills, or a system of rules, or a grammar; it involves an alteration in self-image, the adoption of new social and cultural behaviours and ways of being, and therefore has a significant impact on the social nature of the learner.'
(Marion Williams 1994:77)

Thus, language learning is a deeply social event that requires the incorporation of a wide range of elements of the L2 culture. Accordingly, most research on L2 motivation between the 1960s and 1990s focused on how the students' perceptions of the L2, the L2 speakers and the L2 culture affect their desire to learn the language. This research direction was spearheaded and inspired by a group of social psychologists in Canada, most notably by Robert Gardner, Wallace Lambert and Richard Clément. Because their theory still represents one of the most influential approaches in the L2 field, let us start our exploration of L2 motivation by looking into it in a bit more detail.

The social psychological approach in Canada

It is no accident that L2 motivation research was initiated in Canada. The country is one of the rare bilingual locations in the world where the population is 'officially' divided up to speakers of two powerful *world languages* (English and French). Therefore, the 'competition' between the two official Canadian languages has been particularly fierce. Robert Gardner and his colleagues have proposed that the knowledge of the other community's language might serve as a mediating factor between the two speech communities, which implies that the motivation to learn the language of the other community is a primary force responsible for enhancing or hindering communication and affiliation within Canada. This argument makes intuitive sense and also has turned out to be very saleable to government agencies, resulting in plenty of research money to sponsor work in the field! The initial results obtained by Gardner and Lambert (cf. 1972) were sufficiently powerful to stir up an international interest, and very soon studies of a similar vein were conducted all over the world.

A key tenet of the Canadian social psychological approach is that *attitudes* related to the L2 community (e.g. anglophone learner's feelings about the francophones) exert a strong influence on one's L2 learning. This again makes good sense: as with my experience growing up in Hungary, few learners are likely to be successful in learning the language of a despised community. It is also assumed that language learners' goals fall into two broad categories:

- *Integrative orientation*, which reflects a positive disposition toward the L2 group and the desire to interact with and even become similar to valued members of that community.
- *Instrumental orientation*, where language learning is primarily associated with the potential pragmatic gains of L2 proficiency, such as getting a better job or a higher salary.

Although these two orientations have become widely known in the L2 field, the most elaborate and researched aspect of Gardner's theory is not the integrative/instrumental duality but the broader concept of the *'integrative motive'*. This is a complex construct made up of three main components (see Figure 1 for a schematic representation):

- *integrativeness* (subsuming integrative orientation, interest in foreign languages, and attitudes toward the L2 community);
- *attitudes toward the learning situation* (comprising attitudes toward the teacher and the course);
- *motivation* (made up of motivational intensity, desire to learn the language and attitudes towards learning the language).

As an important addition to Gardner's motivation model, Richard Clément (1980; Clément et al. 1994) has introduced the concept of *linguistic self-confidence* as a significant motivational subsystem, which is very much in line with the increasing importance attached to self-efficacy in mainstream psychological research (as discussed earlier).

The educational shift in the 1990s

The 1990s brought about a change in scholars' thinking about L2 motivation. While no one questioned the significance of the socio-cultural dimension, the general message coming from various parts of the world was that 'there is more to motivation!'. In an influential 'position paper', Graham Crookes and Richard Schmidt (1991: 469) expressed this most explicitly:

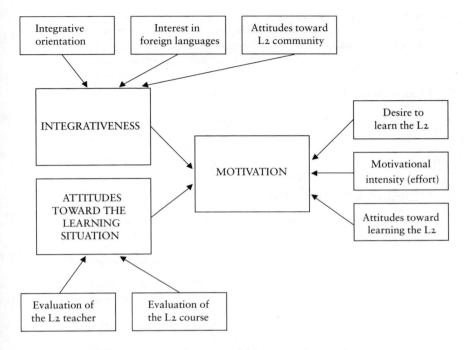

Figure 1 Gardner's conceptualisation of the integrative motive

Discussion of the topic of motivation in second-language (SL)
learning contexts has been limited by the understanding the
field of applied linguistics has attached to it. In that view,
primary emphasis is placed on attitudes and other social
psychological aspects of SL learning. This does not do full
justice to the way SL teachers have used the term motivation.
Their use is more congruent with definitions common outside
social psychology, specifically in education.

That is, researchers in effect wanted to close the gap between motivational theories in educational psychology and in the L2 field, claiming
that by focusing so much on the social dimension, other important
aspects of motivation have been overlooked or played down. As a
result, several extended new L2 motivation constructs were proposed,
all of which provided some sort of a synthesis of old and new elements.
To illustrate the new approaches, let me describe the two most elaborate
frameworks from the period, by Dörnyei (1994) and Williams and
Burden (1997).

Table 2 *Dörnyei's (1994) framework of L2 motivation*

LANGUAGE LEVEL	Integrative motivational subsystem Instrumental motivational subsystem
LEARNER LEVEL	Need for achievement Self-confidence * Language use anxiety * Perceived L2 competence * Causal attributions * Self-efficacy
LEARNING SITUATION LEVEL	
Course-specific motivational components	Interest (in the course) Relevance (of the course to one's needs) Expectancy (of success) Satisfaction (one has in the outcome)
Teacher-specific motivational components	Affiliative motive (to please the teacher) Authority type (controlling vs. autonomy-supporting) Direct socialisation of motivation * Modelling * Task presentation * Feedback
Group-specific motivational Components	Goal-orientedness Norm and reward system Group cohesiveness Classroom goal structure (cooperative, competitive or individualistic)

Dörnyei's 1994 framework of L2 motivation

My 1994 model (see Table 2) is a good example of the 'educational approach', as it specifically focused on motivation from a classroom perspective. It conceptualised L2 motivation in terms of three levels:

- The *Language Level* encompasses various components related to aspects of the L2, such as the culture and the community, as well as the intellectual and pragmatic values and benefits associated with it. That, is, this level represents the traditionally established elements of L2 motivation associated with integrativeness and instrumentality.

- The *Learner Level* involves individual characteristics that the learner brings to the learning process, most notably *self-confidence*, which reflects the influence of Richard Clément's work on the topic.
- The *Learning Situation Level* is associated with situation-specific motives rooted in various aspects of L2 learning within a classroom setting: *course-specific motivational components* (related to the syllabus, the teaching materials, the teaching method and the learning tasks); *teacher-specific motivational components* (concerning the motivational impact of the teacher's personality, behaviour and teaching style/practice); and *group-specific motivational components* (related to the characteristics of the learner group).

Williams and Burden's framework of L2 motivation

Another detailed framework of motivational components was offered by Marion Williams and Bob Burden (1997) (see Table 3) as part of a larger overview of psychology for language teachers. They also considered L2 motivation to be a complex, multi-dimensional construct, but the grouping of the components followed different principles from the Dörnyei (1994) framework. The principal grouping category in the Williams and Burden construct is whether the motivational influence is *internal* or *external*, and within these two categories they distinguished a number of subcomponents, following some current themes in educational psychology.

A process model of language learning motivation

Let me conclude the brief overview of the various motivation theories by presenting a model that I have been working on recently, which reflects a novel approach in L2 motivation research. The construct that I will describe below reflects the principles of a more general and elaborate model devised in collaboration with a friend, István Ottó (Dörnyei and Ottó 1998; Dörnyei 2000, 2001). The new element of the model is that it is based on a *process-oriented approach*. This means that it takes a dynamic view of motivation, trying to account for the *changes of motivation over time*. I believe that this is an important consideration, because when we talk about a prolonged learning activity, such as mastering an L2, motivation cannot be viewed as a stable attribute of learning that remains constant for several months or years. Instead, what most teachers find is that their students' motivation fluctuates, going through certain ebbs and flows. Such variation may be caused by a range of factors, such as the phase of the school year (e.g. motivation might decrease with time) or the type of activity that the

Table 3 *Williams and Burden's (1997) framework of L2 motivation*

INTERNAL FACTORS	EXTERNAL FACTORS

Intrinsic interest of activity
  • arousal of curiosity
  • optimal degree of challenge
Perceived value of activity
  • personal relevance
  • anticipated value of outcomes
  • intrinsic value attributed to the activity
Sense of agency
  • locus of causality
  • locus of control re: process and outcomes
  • ability to set appropriate goals
Mastery
  • feelings of competence
  • awareness of developing skills and mastery in a chosen area
  • self-efficacy
Self-concept
  • realistic awareness of personal strengths and weaknesses in skills required
  • personal definitions and judgements of success and failure
  • self-worth concern
  • learned helplessness
Attitudes
  • to language learning in general
  • to the target language
  • to the target language community and culture
Other affective states
  • confidence
  • anxiety, fear
Developmental age and stage
Gender
	Significant others
	  • parents
	  • teachers
	  • peers
	The nature of interaction with significant others
	  • mediated learning experiences
	  • the nature and amount of feedback
	  • rewards
	  • the nature and amount of appropriate praise
	  • punishments, sanctions
	The learning environment
	  • comfort
	  • resources
	  • time of day, week, year
	  • size of class and school
	  • class and school ethos
	The broader context
	  • wider family networks
	  • the local education system
	  • conflicting interests
	  • cultural norms
	  • societal expectations and attitudes

students face. Therefore, it is my belief that it may be useful to include a time dimension – or a *temporal axis* – in a motivation model that is to be applied to school learning (cf. Dörnyei 2000).

Well said . . .

'within the context of institutionalised learning especially, the common experience would seem to be motivational flux rather than stability.'
(Ema Ushioda 1996:240)

The main assumption underlying our process-oriented approach is that motivation consists of several distinct phases (see Figure 2):

- First it needs to be *generated* – the motivational dimension related to this initial phase can be referred to as *choice motivation*, because the generated motivation leads to the selection of the goal or task to be pursued.
- Second, the generated motivation needs to be actively *maintained* and *protected* while the particular action lasts. This motivational dimension has been referred to as *executive motivation*, and it is particularly relevant to learning in classroom settings, where students are exposed to a great number of distracting influences, such as off-task thoughts, irrelevant distractions from others, anxiety about the tasks, or physical conditions that make it difficult to complete the task.
- Finally, there is a third phase following the completion of the action – termed *motivational retrospection* – which concerns the learners' *retrospective evaluation* of how things went. The way students process their past experiences in this retrospective phase will determine the kind of activities they will be motivated to pursue in the future.

In Figure 2, I listed the main motives that influence the learner's behaviour/thinking during the three phases. These motives include many of the well-known concepts discussed earlier in this chapter. What is important to note about these lists is that the different motivational phases appear to be fuelled by different motives. In agreement with other researchers (e.g. Heckhausen 1991, Williams and Burden 1997) I believe that it involves largely different considerations to deliberate the reasons for doing something and subsequently to decide on a course of action – that is, to *initiate motivation* – from *sustaining motivation*. Although I am not going to elaborate on these motives here, they will re-emerge later in this book because I have used the construct in Figure 2 as

Preactional Stage **Actional Stage** **Postactional Stage**

CHOICE MOTIVATION

Motivational functions:

- Setting goals
- Forming intentions
- Launching action

Main motivational influences:

- Various goal properties (e.g. goal relevance, specificity and proximity)
- Values associated with the learning process itself, as well as with its outcomes and consequences
- Attitudes towards the L2 and its speakers
- Expectancy of success and perceived coping potential
- Learner beliefs and strategies
- Environmental support or hindrance

EXECUTIVE MOTIVATION

Motivational functions:

- Generating and carrying out subtasks
- Ongoing appraisal (of one's achievement)
- Action control (self-regulation)

Main motivational influences:

- Quality of the learning experience (pleasantness, need significance, coping potential, self and social image)
- Sense of autonomy
- Teachers' and parents' influence
- Classroom reward and goal structure (e.g. competitive or cooperative)
- Influence of the learner group
- Knowledge and use of self-regulatory strategies (e.g. goal setting, learning and self-motivating strategies)

MOTIVATIONAL RETROSPECTION

Motivational functions

- Forming causal attributions
- Elaborating standards and strategies
- Dismissing intention & further planning

Main motivational influences:

- Attributional factors (e.g. attributional styles and biases)
- Self-concept beliefs (e.g. self-confidence and self-worth)
- Received feedback, praise, grades

Figure 2 A process model of learning motivation in the L2 classroom

the basis for organising and presenting a systematic overview of motivational strategies. However, to provide some evidence of the process-oriented approach, let me mention here just one observation that many teachers might find familiar and which well illustrates the relevance of such a conception to the study of L2s.

In adult language courses it is not at all uncommon to find people who soon drop out because they realise that they cannot cope with the day-to-day demands of attending the classes and completing the home assignments. What is interesting from our point of view is that some of these learners will decide later to re-enrol in the course; in fact, some learners repeat this cycle several times (which reminds me of anecdotes about married couples who get divorced and then re-marry more than once). Why does this happen? From a process-oriented perspective this behaviour is explainable: enrolling in a course is motivated by 'choice motivation', but the ongoing work that is required during the language course is energised by 'executive motivation'; in the case of drop-outs this latter source of motivation is insufficient. However, once a person has dropped out, the everyday realities of the coursework will be soon forgotten and the more general considerations about the importance of L2 learning become dominant once again – in other words, the person is back to square one and 'choice motivation' comes into force again. The reason why such cycles do not go on ad infinitum (although I have seen people who have quit and then re-started their L2 studies in a seemingly never-ending sequence. . .) is that during the third phase of the motivational cycle – 'motivational retrospection' – most such learners will sooner or later draw the necessary conclusion that even though they value knowing an L2, for various reasons they cannot cope with the actual demands of attending a course.

1.2 Motivating people

A lot has been written on student motivation both in psychology and in L2 studies. Most of this material, however, has been directed at researchers to facilitate further research, rather than at practitioners to facilitate teaching. One reason for this gap between theory and practice is the different nature of the principles that people find useful in educational and research contexts. The kind of knowledge teachers can use best is straightforward and unambiguous, along the lines of 'If you do this, you'll get this'. Psychologists, however, are not very keen on making black-and-white statements because when it comes to humans, there are very few rules and principles that are universally true, regardless of the actual context and purpose of the learning activity. It would be great to have absolute rules such as the ones we find in the natural sciences but in the social sciences nothing is so straightforward and almost everything that has been written in the motivational literature has also been questioned by others. Therefore, motivation researchers in the past have been rather reluctant to come out with sets of practical recommendations for teachers.

Let's face it . . .

'Large numbers of students are rejecting school as a means for improving their lives. Many start by becoming truants at the age of 13 or 14, and then dropping out officially at their first opportunity. Others endure their school years with sullen, glassy-eyed looks on their faces as they slouch in their desks without books, pens, or paper. With two or three notable exceptions, few books are written to help teachers understand these students or deal with the problems of student apathy.'
(James Raffini 1993:xi)

During the last decade, however, things have started to change. More and more articles and books have been published with the word 'motivating' in their title (see the 'Further reading' box at the end of this section), and some of the best-known motivation researchers and educational psychologists have turned their attention to classroom applications. It is as if a new spirit had entered the profession, urging scholars to 'stick their neck out and see what we've got'. And, luckily, what we've got is nothing to be ashamed of. There is a growing set of core knowledge in motivation research that has stood the test of time and which can therefore be safely translated into practical terms. This book is intended to summarise this knowledge. Before launching into the discussion of practical motivational techniques, let me briefly address three general points:

- What exactly do we mean by 'motivating' someone?
- What is the relationship between 'motivating' teaching and 'good' teaching?
- Whose responsibility is it to motivate learners?

What does 'motivating someone' involve?

Motivating someone to do something can involve many different things, from trying to persuade a person directly to exerting indirect influence on him/her by arranging the conditions or circumstances in a way that the person is likely to choose the particular course of action. Sometimes simply providing a good opportunity is enough to do the trick. Whatever form it takes, however, the motivating process is usually a long-term one, built 'one grain of trust and caring at a time' (Scheidecker and Freeman 1999:126). In classroom contexts, in particular, it is rare to find dramatic motivational events that – like a lightening or a revelation – reshape the students' mindsets from one moment to another. Rather, it is typically a series of nuances that might eventually culminate in a long-lasting effect.

Well said . . .

'there are no magic motivational buttons that can be pushed to "make" people want to learn, work hard, and act in a responsible manner. Similarly, no one can be directly "forced" to care about something. . . Facilitation, not control, should be the guiding idea in attempts to motivate humans.'
(Martin Ford 1992:202)

Who can be motivated? Most discussions about motivating techniques are based on the idealistic belief that 'all students are motivated to learn under the right conditions, and that you can provide these conditions in your classroom' (McCombs and Pope 1994:vii). Unfortunately, this assumption is not necessarily true in every case. Realistically, it is highly unlikely that everybody can be motivated to learn everything and even generally motivated students are not equally keen on every subject matter. Yet, my personal belief is in accordance with the spirit of the above statement in that I think that most students' motivation can be 'worked on' and increased. Although rewards and punishments are too often the only tools present in the motivational arsenal of many teachers, the spectrum of other, and potentially more effective, motivational strategies is so broad that it is hard to imagine that none of them would work.

Motivating teaching

I remember a recent experience with a postgraduate student who was writing her MA thesis on how to motivate learners. When she gave me the first draft of the manuscript, I was puzzled to see that a great deal of the material concerned effective teaching in general rather than motivational practices. When I thought about this, however, I realised that she was right in a way. Sometimes the best motivational intervention is

Table 4 *Wlodkowski's (1986: 42) Instructional Clarity Checklist*

1.	Explain things simply.
2.	Give explanations we understand.
3.	Teach at a pace that is not too fast and not too slow.
4.	Stay with a topic until we understand.
5.	Try to find out when we don't understand and then repeat things.
6.	Teach things step-by-step.
7.	Describe the work to be done and how to do it.
8.	Ask if we know what to do and how to do it.
9.	Repeat things when we don't understand.
10.	Explain something and then use an example to illustrate it.
11.	Explain something and then stop so we can ask questions.
12.	Prepare us for what we will be doing next.
13.	Give specific details when teaching or training.
14.	Repeat things that are hard to understand.
15.	Use examples and explain them until we understand.
16.	Explain something and then stop so we can think about it.
17.	Show us how to do the work.
18.	Explain the assignment and the materials we need to do it.
19.	Stress difficult points.
20.	Show examples of how to do course work and assignments.
21.	Give us enough time for practice.
22.	Answer our questions.
23.	Ask questions to find out we understand.
24.	Go over difficult assignments until we understand how to do them.

simply to improve the quality of our teaching. Similarly, no matter how competent a motivator a teacher is, if his/her teaching lacks instructional clarity and the learners simply cannot follow the intended programme, motivation to learn the particular subject matter is unlikely to blossom. Having said that, it is clear that this book cannot cover everything about good teaching. Table 4 contains an inventory of the components that make up instructional quality according to motivational psychologist Raymond Wlodkowski. The techniques listed there are to illustrate the kind of teaching methodological issues which are really important with regard to motivating teaching but which this book is not going to cover.

Whose responsibility is it to motivate learners?

Some of the motivational techniques are closely related to subject-matter teaching (e.g. how to present tasks in a motivating manner – cf.

Section 4.2), whereas others may require extra attention and time (e.g. presenting self-motivating strategies – cf. Section 4.8). Given the reality of constant time pressure in many school contexts, the question of 'Whose job is it to improve motivation?' is a valid one. The current situation is not very promising in this respect: by-and-large, promoting learner motivation is nobody's responsibility. Teachers are supposed to teach the curriculum rather than motivate learners, and the fact that the former cannot happen without the latter is often ignored. For example, I am not aware of a single L2 teacher training programme worldwide in which the development of skills in motivating learners would be a key component of the curriculum.

So, whose responsibility is it to motivate learners? My guess is that it is every teacher's who thinks of the *long-term* development of his/her students. In the short run, preparing for tests might admittedly produce better immediate results than spending some of the time shaping the motivational qualities of the learner group and the individual learners. However, few of us teachers have entered the profession with the sole objective of preparing students for tests . . . Besides, motivational training might be a very good investment in the longer run, and it may also make your own life in the classroom so much more pleasant. As Scheidecker and Freeman (1999:9) succinctly put it, the real reward for motivating teachers is not on pay-day, 'it is when their passion is caught by the students. That is a big-time return on anyone's investment.'

Further reading

During the preparation of this book I have used many sources. Very useful and comprehensive overviews are provided by Jere Brophy's (1998) *Motivating Students to Learn* and Raymond Wlodkowski's (1986) *Enhancing Adult Motivation to Learn*. I have found further valuable material in Brophy (1987), Burden (1995), Canfield and Wells (1994), Covington (1998), Galloway, Rogers, Armstrong and Leo (1998), Good and Brophy (1994), Jones and Jones (1995), Keller (1983), McCombs and Pope (1994), Pintrich and Schunk (1996), Raffini (1993, 1996) and Scheidecker and Freeman (1999). In the L2 field, I am aware of the following works that offer practical motivational ideas and recommendations: Alison (1993), Brown (1994), Chambers (1999), Cranmer (1996), Dörnyei (1994), Dörnyei and Csizér (1998), Oxford and Shearin (1994), and Williams and Burden (1997).

1.3 Motivational strategies

Motivational strategies are techniques that promote the individual's goal-related behaviour. Because human behaviour is rather complex, there are many diverse ways of promoting it – in fact, almost any influence a person is exposed to might potentially affect his/her behaviour. Motivational strategies refer to those *motivational influences that are consciously exerted to achieve some systematic and enduring positive effect.*

With respect to the various strategies promoting classroom L2 learning, there are several ways to organise them into separate 'themes'. We could, for example:

- focus on the *internal structure* of a typical language class and cluster the strategies according to the various structural units (e.g. strategies to present new material, give feedback, set up communicative tasks or assign homework).
- design a primarily *trouble-shooting guide* in which some particularly problematic facets of the classroom's motivational life are listed and suggestions are offered on how to handle these (e.g. how to deal with student lethargy; lack of voluntary participation; or anti-learning influences of deviant children).
- focus on *key motivational concepts* – such as intrinsic interest, self-confidence or student autonomy – and use these as the main organising units.
- centre the discussion on the *main types of teacher behaviour* that have motivating effects (e.g. showing a good example and modelling student behaviour; communication and rapport with the students; consciousness raising about self-regulated strategies; or stage managing classroom events).

Although I believe that all these approaches have their merits, I have chosen to follow a fifth approach which focuses on the different phases of the process-oriented model described earlier (cf. Figure 2 in Section 1.1). The model has been specifically developed for educational applications and it offers an important advantage over the other approaches: *comprehensiveness.* When deliberating on the structure of this book, it seemed to me that following through the motivational process from the initial arousal of the motivation to the completion and evaluation of the motivated action is in many ways more logical than making somewhat arbitrary decisions about which central themes the material should be built around.

Key units in this process-oriented organisation include:

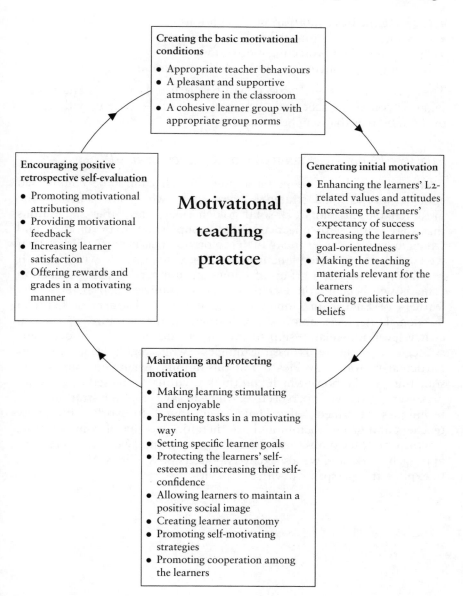

Figure 3 The components of motivational teaching practice in the L2 classroom

- Creating the basic motivational conditions.
- Generating initial motivation.
- Maintaining and protecting motivation.
- Encouraging positive retrospective self-evaluation.

These four motivational aspects will be discussed in one chapter each. Figure 3 contains a schematic representation of the system, with details of the sub-areas that will be covered.

Final words: not every strategy works in every context!

Finally, I would like to make a point which cannot be emphasised enough: motivational strategies, even those which are generally the most reliable, are not rock-solid golden rules, but rather suggestions that may work with one teacher or group better than another, and which may work better today than tomorrow. This is particularly true if we consider how varied language learning situations are worldwide. It is unlikely that, say, a group of immigrant mothers studying French in Canada will benefit from exactly the same strategies as primary school learners of English in Hong Kong or university learners of Latin in Sweden. Differences amongst the learners in their culture, age, proficiency level and relationship to the target language may render some strategies completely useless/meaningless, while highlighting others as particularly prominent. Please bear this in mind when you come across something in the book which you think is culturally biased or does not make sense from your perspective. All I can say is that the strategies and techniques described below have been found to work with many teachers and groups before and are therefore worthy of consideration. To turn to McCombs and Pope (1994) again: 'We have seen this approach work, and we are excited about its possibilities. We invite you to explore this perspective with us' (p. vii).

2 Creating the basic motivational conditions

Motivational strategies cannot be employed successfully in a 'motivational vacuum' – certain preconditions must be in place before any further attempts to generate motivation can be effective. In my experience, the following three motivational conditions in particular are indispensable:

- appropriate teacher behaviours and a good relationship with the students;
- a pleasant and supportive classroom atmosphere;
- a cohesive learner group with appropriate group norms.

Of course, the three conditions are interrelated because, for example, you cannot have a pleasant classroom climate if there is tension between you and the students, but it is useful to look at them one by one.

2.1 Appropriate teacher behaviours

In 1998, Kata Csizér and I conducted a survey (Dörnyei and Csizér 1998) among Hungarian teachers of English to find out what they thought of various motivational techniques and how often they used them in their own teaching practice. In order to even out the different personal views, we included a relatively large number of practitioners (N = 200) from diverse contexts (ranging from primary school instructors teaching beginners to university lecturers teaching English majors) and then summarised their responses. The survey revealed that the participants considered the teacher's own behaviour to be the single most important motivational tool. Furthermore, the results also exposed that this 'tool' was one of the most under-utilised motivational resources in the teacher's classroom practice. A year later I was interested to read a study by Gary Chambers (1999) that was conducted in a different context, amongst British secondary school learners of

German, and which led the author to the same conclusion: of all the factors that were hypothesised to contribute to the pupils' positive or negative appraisal of L2 learning, the teacher came out on top for all the age groups surveyed.

From an interview with a trainee teacher of English . . .

'When do you think that things started to change?'

'You mean, when did I decide that I wanted this for my career? Well, I started to like English when I was in high school. I started to enjoy it a little bit more because of a teacher I had. She was really, ah, a role model for me, you know. The way she taught us, it was really great. And that made me love this language and that made me understand that, "OK, now I want to be an English teacher".'

(Adapted from Silva 2001)

These results, of course, only confirm what most experienced teachers already know, namely that almost everything a teacher does in the classroom has a motivational influence on students. Because this book is primarily about what you as a teacher can do to motivate your learners, the issue of appropriate teacher behaviours will be regularly addressed throughout. Here, I will discuss four general points. The teacher's:

- enthusiasm;
- commitment to and expectations for the students' learning;
- relationship with the students;
- relationship with the students' parents.

Enthusiasm

Who have been your most influential teachers? Who do you still remember as someone who has made a difference in your life? These are the questions that American psychologist Mihaly Csikszentmihalyi (1997) has addressed in a thought-provoking article, and his answer was that it is the enthusiastic ones. The ones who love their subject matter and who show by their dedication and their passion that there is nothing else on earth they would rather be doing. They are the 'nutcases' whose involvement in their areas of expertise is so excessive that it is bordering on being crazy. Students might make fun of this dedication but deep inside, argues Csikszentmihalyi, they admire that passion. Such a commitment towards the subject matter then becomes 'infectious', instilling in students a similar willingness to pursue knowledge.

Well said . . .

'Young people are more intelligent than adults generally give them credit for. They can usually discern, for instance, whether an adult they know likes or dislikes what he or she is doing. If a teacher does not believe in his job, does not enjoy the learning he is trying to transmit, the student will sense this and derive the entirely rational conclusion that the particular subject matter is not worth mastering for its own sake.'
(Mihaly Csikszentmihalyi 1997:77)

Many scholars share Csikszentmihalyi's belief that enthusiasm for one's specialisation area and the ability to make this enthusiasm public rather than hiding it is one of the most important ingredients of motivationally successful teaching. Projecting enthusiasm is related to the more general process of *modelling*, which is a very effective method of teaching various things by setting an example, and there is no reason why this example could not involve motivational factors such as effort expenditure, positive attitudes and interest in the subject (cf. Brophy and Kher 1986). On the other hand, we must also bear in mind that different cultures consider the expression of personal feelings – such as enthusiasm – differently, and what would be a highly motivating personal example in one country might be looked upon as rather 'uncultured' in another.

It is also important to stress that projecting enthusiasm does not mean pep talks, theatrical performance or tears in our eyes when we utter the words 'Shakespeare' or 'past conditional'. Rather, as Good and Brophy (1994) argue, it means that we clearly identify our reasons for being interested in the topic and then *share* these with the students. Dramatic salesmanship might work if you are that sort of person but low-key, sincere statements will be just as effective.

Strategy 1

Demonstrate and talk about your own enthusiasm for the course material, and how it affects you personally.

More specifically:

- Share your own personal interest in the L2 with your students.
- Show students that you value L2 learning as a meaningful experience that produces satisfaction and enriches your life.

Commitment to and expectations for the students' academic progress

In his/her position of group leader, the teacher embodies the class spirit. Broadly speaking, if you show commitment towards the students' learning and progress, there is a very good chance that they will do the same thing. It is important that everybody in the classroom should be aware that you care; that you are not there just for the salary; that it is important for you that your students succeed; that you are ready to work just as hard as the students towards this success. Of course, these phrases do sound a bit trite, just like the three Musketeers' motto, 'All for one and one for all!'. However, my experience is that this aspect of teacher behaviour cannot be overemphasised because students are extremely sensitive to the cues coming from the teacher.

There are many ways of expressing that the students' learning matters to you. They include:

- offering concrete assistance;
- offering to meet students individually to explain things;
- responding immediately when help is requested;
- correcting tests and papers promptly;
- sending learners copies of relevant/particularly interesting articles;
- arranging extracurricular instructional programmes/opportunities;
- encouraging extra assignments and offering to assist with these;
- showing concern when things aren't going well;
- allowing students to call you at home when they have a problem (Hmm. . .);
- being available for overtime (Hmmmm. . .).

If students can sense that the teacher doesn't care . . .

. . . this perception is the fastest way to undermine their motivation. The spiritual (and sometimes physical) absence of the teacher sends such a powerful message of 'It doesn't matter!' to the students, that everybody, even the most dedicated ones, are likely to be affected and become demoralised.

Jere Brophy (1998) adds a further important ingredient to the commitment issue. He emphasises that in our communication with the students we should take it for granted that the students share our enthusiasm for learning. We should make explicit references to this. In this way, as

Brophy argues, 'To the extent that you *treat students as if they already are eager learners*, they are more likely to become eager learners. Let them know that they are expected to be curious . . .' (p. 170).

Teacher expectations

The need to expect learners to show interest in order for this to really happen is an example of the more general issue of *teacher expectations*. It has been shown by a convincing amount of research that it is not enough to be merely committed to the students' academic progress, you also need to have sufficiently high expectations for what the students can achieve. For example, in one of the most famous experiments in educational psychology, Rosenthal and Jacobson (1968) administered an intelligence test to primary school children at the start of the academic year. Teachers were told that the purpose of this test was to predict which students would 'bloom' intellectually during the academic year. The researchers, however, deceived the teachers because instead of providing them with the true test scores, they identified 20 per cent of the sample as potential 'intellectual bloomers' randomly, that is, regardless of their actual intellectual potential. The results of the experiment were quite remarkable: by the end of the year there were significant differences between the 'bloomers' and the control students whereas at the beginning of the year they were similar in every respect except in the way they were labelled by the researchers.

Rosenthal and Jacobson (1968) explained the emerging difference by arguing that the (false) information about the students created differential teacher expectations concerning them and these expectations acted as *self-fulfilling prophecies* in that students lived up to them (this effect has also been referred to as the 'Pygmalion effect' after Bernard Shaw's play). In other words, if you yourself believe that your students can reach high levels of achievement, there is a good chance that they will too. However, if you have low expectations about how much your students can cope with, they will probably 'live down' to these expectations. This means, for example, that ability grouping is a dangerous practice because teachers who are to teach the low-ability groups are bound to be influenced by this knowledge, which may send the children on an ever downward spiral of low achievement and low expectations.

> **Strategy 2**
>
> *Take the students' learning very seriously.*
>
> More specifically:
>
> - Show students that you care about their progress.
> - Indicate your mental and physical availability for all things academic.
> - Have sufficiently high expectations for what your students can achieve.

Good relationship with the students

I don't think it requires much justification to claim that it is important for a motivating teacher to have a positive relationship with the students on a personal and not just on an academic level. In fact, a lot of the previous section could be simply copied here by replacing the phrase 'care for the students' learning' with 'care for the students as real people'. Teachers who share warm, personal interactions with their students, who respond to their concerns in an empathic manner and who succeed in establishing relationships of mutual trust and respect with the learners, are more likely to inspire them in academic matters than those who have no personal ties with the learners. Of course, this again is a highly culture-sensitive issue.

> **Well said . . .**
>
> 'Building trust in a classroom is a slow process and results from many small incidents in which the teacher has responded honestly and dependably. It is easy to trust "trustable" students, but it is the "untrustable" students who need systematic trust-building experiences. . . . While some students may occasionally abuse their trust, they need repeated opportunities to learn and practise this character trait.'
> (James Raffini 1993:145–6)

Developing a personal relationship with the students and achieving their respect is easier said than done. It is a gradual process built on a foundation whose components include the teacher's:

- acceptance of the students,
- ability to listen and pay attention to them,
- availability for personal contact.

Acceptance

Acceptance is one of the three linchpins of Carl Rogers' humanistic psychology (the other two being 'empathy' and 'congruence'), which has been very influential in the development of student-centred teaching in general (cf. Rogers and Freiberg 1994). It involves a non-judgemental positive attitude, something like the way we may feel towards a relative, for example an aunt or uncle, who has his/her shortcomings but whom we know well and is one of us. It is not to be confused with approval; we may accept a person without necessarily approving of everything he/she does. It is a bit like 'loving the sinner, not the sin'. Let me include here an illustration of what acceptance involves that I have heard recently (and sorry if you are already familiar with it). It is about a picture not unlike the one below. The question was: 'What can you see?' When I first saw this picture, I saw a black line across a white rectangle. But the person who presented the picture said that it was, in fact, two white triangles next to each other . . . If you accept someone, you try and focus on the white triangles rather than the black lines.

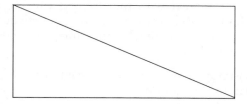

Ability to listen and pay attention to students

According to Wlodkowski (1986:28), *listening* to a person is the 'single most powerful transaction that occurs between ourselves and another person that tells that individual that we accept him as a human being . . . The way we listen tells learners more than anything else how much consideration we are really giving them'. That is, students need to feel that you pay personal attention to them. Of course, everybody will understand that with a whole class to look after, you cannot spend too much time with individual students, but there is a whole variety of small gestures that do not take up much time which can convey personal attention and can touch the lives of every student in some way (cf. Burden 1995:224; Raffini 1996:182). For example:

- Greet students and remember their names.
- Smile at them.
- Notice interesting features of their appearance (e.g. new haircut).
- Learn something unique about each student and occasionally mention it to them.
- Ask them about their lives outside school.
- Show interest in their hobbies.
- Express in your comments that you've thought about them and that their individual effort is recognised.
- Refer back to what you have talked about before.
- Recognise birthdays.
- Move around in class.
- Include personal topics and examples about students in discussing content matters.
- Send notes/homework to absent students.

Availability

Availability is a difficult issue at a time when most teachers around the world are overburdened and pressed for time. There is no question that individual personal contact with the students can do wonders to our relationship with them. But how can we find the time necessary for this? Well, even if we do not have much extra time, we might be able to do some of the following:

- Join students for lunch in the school canteen (if there is one).
- Join students in the playground.
- Chaperone school events.
- Give them your home telephone number for times when they need assistance.
- Give them your e-mail address (if you work in an area where the internet is available) and encourage them to write to you.
- Set a weekly slot when you are in your office/staff room in case someone wants/needs to talk to you.

> **Strategy 3**
>
> *Develop a personal relationship with your students.*
>
> More specifically:
>
> - Show students that you accept and care about them.
> - Pay attention and listen to each of them.
> - Indicate your mental and physical availability.

Good relationship with the parents

Something we may easily forget is that our good relationship with the students also depends on our good relationship with their parents (this section, of course, does not much apply to adult education). For most children their parents' opinion matters, and therefore parents can be powerful allies in any motivational effort. Brophy (1998) points out that one of the most distinctive features of teachers who have been successful with hard-to-reach, at-risk students is that they reach out to these students' families, get to know them, keep them informed of what is going on at school, and involve them in decision-making. In other words, they enlist the parents as allies in their attempts to make a difference in the children's lives. Such a collaborative relationship might be hard to establish to start with, but – in Brophy's experience – most parents care about their children's success at school and will respond positively if they feel that the teacher is acting in their children's best interest. In fact, the reason why many parents fail to perform their supportive role is because – due to a lack of positive models in their own childhood – they simply do not realise the importance of such support or know how to provide it.

Gardner (1985) further argues that with regard to L2 learning the parents also play a 'passive role', which involves *indirect* modelling and communicating their attitudes towards L2 learning and the L2 community. Children are normally well aware of what their parents *really* think of the L2 and its speakers. Gardner presents evidence that this passive role can be very powerful even at times when the parent seemingly supports the child's academic progress (e.g. checks their homework). If the parent harbours latent negative/critical attitudes towards the L2 community, the child is likely to pick up the negative message, which will undermine motivation. This is often the case with the children of those expatriates who compare their often temporary home unfavourably with their home country and do not make any attempt to learn the L2 of the host nation themselves. Even if they would like their children to master the local language, this may not actually happen because of the conflicting messages the children receive.

> **Strategy 4**
>
> *Develop a collaborative relationship with the students' parents.*
>
> More specifically:
>
> - Keep parents regularly informed about their children's progress.
> - Ask for their assistance in performing certain supportive tasks at home.

2.2 A pleasant and supportive atmosphere in the classroom

Language learning is one of the most face-threatening school subjects because of the pressure of having to operate using a rather limited language code. Learners are forced to 'babble like a child' which might just be the last straw for some whose personal identity is already unstable or damaged. In a language class learners need to take considerable risk even to produce relatively simple answers/statements because it is all too easy to make a mistake when you have to pay attention to pronunciation, intonation, grammar *and* content at the same time. No wonder that language anxiety has been found to be a powerful factor hindering L2 learning achievement (MacIntyre 1999; Young 1999). The solution, according to the general consensus amongst motivation researchers, is straightforward: We need to create a pleasant and supportive classroom atmosphere. Indeed, in the Hungarian teacher survey mentioned before, the importance of the classroom climate as a motivational tool was rank ordered second (after the teacher's own behaviour) amongst all the motivational dimensions. So the question is: how can we create a pleasant and supportive classroom atmosphere?

The ideal classroom climate . . .

It is easy to tell when the 'pleasant-and-supportive-classroom-atmo-sphere' is there – you can sense it after only a few minutes' stay in the particular class. There is no tension in the air; students are at ease; there are no sharp – let alone hostile – comments made to ridicule each other. There are no put-downs or sarcasm. Instead, there is mutual trust and respect. No need for anyone to feel anxious or insecure. Scheidecker and Freeman (1999:138) have summarised very expressively the essence of the classroom with a motivational climate for learning: When one watches students enter such a classroom, 'one gets an overwhelming sense that the students shed emotional baggage at the doorway'. This is an 'emotional safe zone'.

The psychological environment of the classroom is made up of a number of different components. One of these, the *teacher's rapport with the students*, has already been discussed. A second constituent, the *students' relationship with each other*, will be addressed in the next section, along with the question of classroom rules and norms. What is important to mention here is that in a safe and supportive classroom the *norm of tolerance* prevails and students feel comfortable taking risks because they know that they will not be embarrassed or criticised if they make a mistake. It has been made clear to them that mistakes are a natural part of learning (for more details about this aspect of the classroom climate, see Section 4.4 on 'Protecting the learners' self-esteem and increasing their self-confidence').

A further tool to improve the classroom atmosphere is the use of *humour*. This is a very potent factor, yet it is often ignored in theoretical writings on motivation. I do not know whether this is because in their rigorous and disciplined quest for truth many researchers have simply forgotten what humour is or because scholars are reluctant to promote a feature – the sense of humour – that they think not everybody has or can acquire. The main point about having humour in the classroom is not so much about continuously cracking jokes but rather having a relaxed attitude about how seriously we take ourselves. If students can sense that the teacher allows a healthy degree of self-mockery and does not treat school as the most hallowed of all places, the jokes will come.

Finally, we should not forget that the classroom is not only a psychological but also a *physical* environment. The classroom atmo-sphere will be strongly influenced by the decoration: posters, bulletin board displays, flowers, funny objects ('the puppet of the class') are all welcome. Some teachers (and many school authorities) may not agree with me, but I have also found soft drinks, snacks and music before and after class (and during some L2 tasks) to be successful in creating a more relaxed atmosphere. The most important thing, however, is not the aesthetic qualities of the surroundings themselves but rather the extent to which the students are involved in personalising the classroom. This is related to the abstract notion of the *ownership of the classroom.* Personalising the classroom can be seen as students exercising increasing control over their environment; therefore, we might encourage learners to 'take over' some control over the walls, spatial arrangement of the furniture, background music, etc.

Strategy 5

Create a pleasant and supportive atmosphere in the classroom.

More specifically (in addition to suggestions mentioned in other sections of this chapter):

- Establish a norm of tolerance.
- Encourage risk-taking and have mistakes accepted as a natural part of learning.
- Bring in and encourage humour.
- Encourage learners to personalise the classroom environment according to their taste.

2.3 A cohesive learner group with appropriate group norms

Have you ever taught a class in which there were such strong cliques and hostile feelings amongst the learners that they simply could not concentrate on the tasks? Have you ever had a group of learners amongst whom it was simply not done to look keen, and anyone who showed the slightest enthusiasm towards the subject was quickly labelled a 'brain', a 'nerd', a 'creep' or a 'swot'? If you have, you will know from bitter experience that the characteristics of your class group make a lot of difference when it comes to the students' attitudes towards learning. Indeed, it is a well established fact in social psychology that the 'group' as a social unit exerts a powerful influence on its members' behaviour; there is even a whole discipline, *group dynamics*, which is entirely devoted to the study of how groups behave and develop.

While I believe that the knowledge about group behaviour that group dynamics can offer is extremely relevant to language teachers (see Dörnyei and Malderez 1997, 1999; and Ehrman and Dörnyei 1998, for detailed discussions), here I will only highlight two aspects of group dynamics that have direct motivational bearings: *group cohesiveness* and *group norms*. Following these discussions I will briefly address the sensitive issue of how to discipline students without losing our motivational objectives.

Creating a cohesive learner group

A cohesive learner group is one which is 'together'; in which there is a strong 'we' feeling; and which students are happy to belong to. That is, cohesiveness refers to the members' commitment to the group and to each other. It is the 'magnetism' or 'glue' that holds the group together. Cohesiveness is often manifested by members seeking each other out, providing mutual support, and making each other welcome in the group (Ehrman and Dörnyei 1998). What is even more important from our perspective is that student motivation tends to increase in cohesive class groups. This is due to the fact that in such groups students share an increased responsibility for achieving the group goals, they 'pull each other along' and the positive relations among them make the learning process more enjoyable in general.

> *Well said . . .*
>
> 'While there are too few rewards in school teaching, one of the most satisfying is the pride of accomplishment that comes from teaching in a classroom that has developed this level of cohesiveness.'
> (James Raffini 1993:95)

Whether or not a class becomes a cohesive community is not simply a question of luck. There are a number of specific factors that can positively contribute to the process, and many of these are within the teacher's control. In the following, I will list ten important factors along with some practical examples and suggestions (see Ehrman and Dörnyei 1998, for more details).

1. The *amount of time spent together* and the *shared group history*: there isn't much you can do about this one . . .
2. The extent to which group members can *learn about each other*: In order to help learners to get to know each other better, you can include special 'ice-breaking activities' at the beginning of a new course. These are designed to set members at ease, get them to

memorise each other's names, and to share personal information. Later on in the course you can provide further opportunities for students to learn more about each other by personalising certain language tasks or by choosing, in preference, activities with a potential for eliciting genuine personal information.

3. *Proximity* (i.e. physical distance such as sitting next to each other), *contact* and *interaction*: You may want to move students round from time to time to prevent the emergence of rigid seating patterns. Also, activities such as pair work, small group work, role-play and project work are very effective in allowing people to come into contact and interact with one another. Extracurricular activities and outings are also good ways of providing opportunities for contact and interaction.

4. *Cooperation* between members for common goals: student collaboration can be successfully promoted by including certain tasks – such as role-play performances, problem solving activities, project work, filling in worksheets, and preparing group reports – which require the preparation of a single 'group product' (see Section 4.6, for more details).

5. *The rewarding nature of group experience*: a commonplace yet true is that the more people enjoy the learning process in the class, the more they will want to belong to the class (see Section 4.1, for more).

6. *Successful completion of whole-group tasks* and a sense of group achievement: you may occasionally include whole-group tasks or projects which generate a satisfying visible product, or conclude in the solving of a puzzle or problem – after which the group can congratulate themselves on their achievement.

7. *Intragroup competition*: small group 'fun' competitions (i.e. games in which small groups compete with each other) promote inter-member relationships. You may want to put students together who would not normally make friends easily.

8. *Common threat* (e.g. the feeling of fellowship before a difficult exam) or *joint hardship* that group members have experienced (e.g. carrying out some tough task together): these create solidarity among the 'fellow-sufferers', but I am not sure how far we can take the practical implications of this . . .

9. *Group legends*: you may promote the building of a kind of 'group mythology' by encouraging learners to give the group a name and to invent characteristics for it. They may also establish group rituals, create a semi-official group history, prepare 'group objects' and symbols (such as flags or coats of arms) and find or create appropriate group mottoes/logos.

10. *Investing in the group*: it has been found that when members spend a considerable amount of time and effort contributing to the group goals, this will increase their commitment towards these goals. Therefore eliciting some significant investment early in the group's life may work towards group cohesiveness.

Strategy 6

Promote the development of group cohesiveness.

More specifically:

- Try and promote interaction, cooperation and the sharing of genuine personal information among the learners.
- Use ice-breakers at the beginning of a course.
- Regularly use small-group tasks where students can mix.
- Encourage and if possible organise extracurricular activities and outings.
- Try and prevent the emergence of rigid seating patterns.
- Include activities that lead to the successful completion of whole-group tasks or involve small-group competition games.
- Promote the building of a group legend.

Establishing constructive group norms

In every classroom there is a range of subtle and less subtle rules that determine what students can and cannot do. The interesting thing about these 'group norms' is that only some of them have been mandated by the teacher (e.g. 'No eating in class!'), others have spontaneously developed during the course of the group's development and are not even explicitly stated (e.g. the kind of jokes allowed or clothes worn). In many contemporary classrooms we can, regrettably, find the covert 'norm of mediocrity', which results in learners suffering social consequences for academic success. In such contexts, a student's lack of motivation can often be traced back to a real or imagined fear of being isolated or rejected by their peers. On the other hand, if the group adopts effective learning-oriented norms, this can be a major contribution to group motivation.

How can we establish constructive group norms? After all, everybody, teachers and students alike, would agree that there need to be certain 'rules of conduct' in the classroom to make joint learning possible. In

Table 5 *Sample set of class rules*

═══

For the students:

- Let's not be late for class.
- Always write your homework.
- Once a term you can 'pass', i.e. say that you haven't prepared.
- In small group work only the L2 can be used.
- If you miss a class, make up for it and ask for the homework.

For the teacher:

- The class should finish on time.
- Homework and tests should be marked within a week.
- Always give advance notice of a test.

For everybody:

- Let's try and listen to each other.
- Let's help each other.
- Let's respect each other's ideas and values.
- It's OK to make mistakes: they are learning points.
- Let's not make fun of each other's weaknesses.
- We must avoid hurting each other, verbally or physically.

═══

my own teaching experience I have come to agree with research findings that suggest that norms are most efficient if they are *explicitly discussed* and *willingly adopted* by members. To facilitate this, I have often included an explicit *norm-building procedure* early in the group's life by

- formulating potential norms;
- justifying their purpose in order to enlist support for them;
- having them discussed by the whole group;
- eliciting further potential norms from the learners and subjecting these to discussion too;
- and finally agreeing on a mutually accepted set of 'class rules'.

Such a procedure can take the form of a negotiated pyramid discussion, for example, first students discuss a particular point in pairs, then two pairs come together and come to an agreement, then they pool their ideas in groups of eight, etc. The consequences for violating any formally agreed norm should also be specified, and it is a good idea to put the established class rules (and the consequences for violating them) on display on a wall chart. Table 5 presents a sample set of class rules.

There is one thing I would like to emphasise concerning class norms.

Learners are very sensitive to the teacher's attitude towards these norms: as mentioned earlier, teachers, through their position as designated leaders, embody 'group conscience', and the model they set by their behaviour plays a powerful role in shaping the class. The saying 'Practise what you preach' is very relevant here: if the teacher does not pay enough attention to the enforcement of the established norms, learners very soon get the message that those rules are not really important and will rapidly discount and disobey them. For example, if the group has originally agreed on always writing their homework but the teacher sometimes forgets to check this or lets those who have failed to complete theirs get away too easily, the homework-writing morale of the class will soon plummet.

Strategy 7

Formulate group norms explicitly, and have them discussed and accepted by the learners.

More specifically:

- Include a specific 'group rules' activity at the beginning of a group's life to establish the norms explicitly.
- Explain the importance of the norms you mandate and how they enhance learning, and ask for the students' agreement.
- Elicit suggestions for additional rules from the learners and discuss these in the same way as the rules you have proposed.
- Put the group rules (and the consequences for violating them) on display.

How to discipline learners who break the rules

Strictly speaking, discipline is not so much a motivational as a classroom management issue (which falls outside the scope of this book). Yet, it is often at times of conflict that our carefully constructed motivational practice collapses, so it might be important to say a few words about how to discipline students in a motivational (or at least not de-motivational) manner.

From the perspective of group dynamics, the best method of discipline is to leave it to the students themselves. This may not be as unrealistic as it first sounds. The advantage of well-chosen and fully accepted norms (discussed above) is exactly that group members tend to abide by them without much pressure being exerted, and when someone violates the class norms, the group is likely to be able to cope with such deviations. In her influential book on group work, Elisabeth Cohen (1994:60) summarises very well the importance of a successfully developed norm system in educational settings:

> the fact that new norms have been internalised is of consider-able practical importance. Much of the work that teachers usually do is taken care of by the students themselves; the group makes sure that everyone understands what to do; the group helps to keep everyone on task; group members assist one another. Instead of the teacher having to control everyone's behaviour, the students take charge of themselves and others.

The power of the group . . .

We should not underestimate the power of the class group to cope with people who break the rules. They can bring to bear consider-able group pressure on errant members, by:

- showing active support for the teacher;
- indirectly expressing disapproval with shifts in eye contact, with-drawal from interaction;
- openly ridiculing or criticising the violator;
- putting the violator in 'social quarantine'.

Let us not forget that group pressure can be powerful enough to make certain students depressed, sometimes suicidal, and groups can also drive teachers crazy if they choose to . . .

Unfortunately, there will be times when the group won't do the job for us and we must confront students about misbehaviour. At times like this, the rule of thumb generally mentioned in the literature is that we should address the issue directly, trying to discuss with the students involved what they can do to engage in more positive behaviour. This may be easier if we manage to separate students from their actions in the spirit of 'I accept you but not your behaviour'. McCombs and Pope (1994:40) argue that, contrary to belief, most misbehaviour in the classroom is the result of the students' low self-esteem: 'Students, rather than being malicious, attention-seeking egomaniacs, are misbehaving because they're scared or insecure'. In any case, if any disciplining is necessary, it should be fair, well-understood by the 'victim' and con-sistently applied. Easier said than done.

Strategy 8

Have the group norms consistently observed.

More specifically:

- Make sure that you yourself observe the established norms consistently.
- Never let any violations go unnoticed.

3 Generating initial motivation

Psychologists often view little children as motivationally 'innocent' and 'uncorrupted' because they seem to possess a natural curiosity about the world and an inherent desire to learn. This is, in fact, often cited as a proof that motivation to learn, just like the ability to acquire language, is an innate characteristic of the human species. Therefore, in an ideal world where the learners' curiosity and inherent motivation has not as yet been curbed or diminished by a student-unfriendly school system, all learners are eager to learn and the learning experience is a constant source of intrinsic pleasure for them.

Classroom teachers in primary and secondary schools, however, tend to have perceptions that are in a sharp contrast with this idyllic view. Instead of all those keen pupils who – according to the theory – should be eagerly absorbing the morsels of wisdom offered to them, what they can see is rather reluctant youngsters who are totally unaware of the fact that there should be an innate curiosity in them, let alone a desire to learn. The regrettable fact is that if school children could freely choose what to do, academic learning for many would most likely feature very low on their agenda. Let's face it: school attendance is compulsory, and the content of the curriculum is almost always selected on the basis of what society – rather than the learners themselves – considers important (Brophy, 1998). Furthermore, it is also difficult for the students who are in the most energetic years of their lives to spend what seem to them terribly long periods of time confined to the relatively small space of the classroom, and the fact that they are continuously monitored and assessed does not add to their well-being either. It is no wonder, therefore, that in a large-scale US survey Csikszentmihalyi and his colleagues (Schneider, Csikszentmihalyi and Knauth 1995; Wong and Csikszentmihalyi 1991) have found that schoolwork was considered to be the *least* rewarding activity among adolescents, and the most common adjectives they used to describe their classroom experience were 'boring', 'unenjoyable' and 'constrained'.

Thus, as Jere Brophy (1998) argues, while inborn curiosity and the intrinsic pleasure of learning are certainly noble and commendable concepts, if we really wish to say something of classroom relevance, we need to adopt a more down-to-earth perspective. For most teachers the real motivational issue is to find ways to encourage their students to accept the goals of the given classroom activities, regardless of whether or not the students enjoy these activities or would choose to engage in them if other alternatives were available. Unless you are singularly fortunate with the composition of your class group, student motivation will not be automatically there and you will need to try and actively generate positive student attitudes towards learning. This is true even if the basic motivational conditions discussed in the previous chapter are in place.

3.1 Enhancing the learners' language-related values and attitudes

It is appropriate to start the discussion of building motivation with the question of *values*. Everybody from a very young age onwards has a fairly well-established value system consisting of a collection of attitudes, beliefs and feelings related to the world around us and who we are in it. This value system is the outcome of our upbringing and our past experiences, and it plays a powerful role in our lives: it largely determines our basic preferences and approaches to activities. Therefore, the most far-reaching consequences in motivating L2 learners can be achieved by promoting positive language-related values and attitudes. In the following I will distinguish three relatively separate value dimensions – attitudes and values related to the:

- actual process of learning the target language – *intrinsic value*;
- target language itself and its speakers – *integrative value*;
- consequences and benefits of having learnt the target language – *instrumental value*.

Before we look at these three areas separately, let me briefly address a general question that is related to all three dimensions: How difficult is it to modify one's value system? After all, given that this system has developed through long years of exposure to varied world experiences, isn't it an illusion for us, teachers, to expect to be able to make lasting changes in it? This is indeed a valid concern but there is some hope. Although values cannot be transmitted directly through traditional instruction, they can be *socialised* rather effectively through three processes:

- exposure to respected models who exhibit them;
- persuasive communication;
- participation in powerful learning experiences.

Of these processes, let me highlight here the first one – *modelling* – which is held to be one of the most powerful ways of teaching in general.

Well said . . .

'We know that heroines and heroes, intellectual and financial wizards, and people in high and low places in histories, stories and society inspire us throughout our lives with their deeds and ideas.'
(Tim Murphey 1998a:205)

In Section 2.1, I have already discussed one example of modelling in the classroom, namely the process of teachers demonstrating enthusiasm and commitment, thereby 'infecting' their students. However, Tim Murphey (1998a) argues convincingly that teachers may not always be the ideal role models, because they are too different from their students both in age and social position. Instead, he recommends that we use for the purpose of modelling various desirable attitudes and practices of some 'lesser gods, closer to home' such as the students' 'near peer role models'. Near peer role models are peers who are close to the learners' social, professional and/or age level (and are preferably of the same sex), and whom for some reason they may respect or admire. The particularly strong impact of these 'lesser gods' is due to the fact that their admired features seem more prominent and more possible to imitate since in many ways these people are already very similar to the students. Therefore, as Murphey has found, if you can find some potential near peer role models and present them to your students (either in person or on video), this may make a lasting impression on some of the learners. For this reason, he has regularly invited successful older students to visit his classes, and has also organised projects whereby his learners interviewed other students about how they coped with certain language-related difficulties. He found that printing student comments in a class newsletter, or collecting language learner histories in a booklet, was also highly inspirational.

> **Strategy 9**
>
> *Promote the learners' language-related values by presenting peer role models.*
>
> More specifically:
>
> - Invite senior students to talk to your class about their positive experiences.
> - Feedback to the students the views of their peers, e.g. in the form of a class newsletter.
> - Associate your learners with peers (e.g. in group or project work) who are enthusiastic about the subject.

The intrinsic value of L2 learning

The *intrinsic value* of L2 learning is associated with the learners' interest in and anticipated enjoyment of the language learning activity. The key issue in generating interest is to 'whet the students' appetite', that is, to arouse the students' curiosity and attention and to create an attractive image for the course. This is very much a 'selling' task in which you may:

- point out challenging, exotic or satisfying aspects of L2 learning;
- connect L2 learning with activities that students already find interesting or hold in esteem (e.g. computer-assisted learning);
- highlight the variety of activities that L2 learning may involve; and
- provide a demonstration of some particularly enjoyable tasks.

Because first impressions are important, it is vital to make the first encounter with the L2 as positive as possible; this impression, once formed, will strongly influence how learners will anticipate future experiences with the subject (Wlodkowski 1986).

> **Strategy 10**
>
> *Raise the learners' intrinsic interest in the L2 learning process.*
>
> More specifically:
>
> - Highlight and demonstrate aspects of L2 learning that your students are likely to enjoy.
> - Make the first encounters with the L2 a positive experience.

Integrative values related to the L2 and its speakers

The term 'integrativeness' may sound a bit odd when you first come across it, yet this term has made a remarkable career in L2 motivation research. First introduced by Robert Gardner and his associates in Canada (see Section 1.1), the concept does not necessarily concern any sort of *real* integration into anything. Instead, in most cases it refers to a *metaphorical* integration, reflecting the 'individual's willingness and interest in social interaction with members of other groups' (Gardner and MacIntyre 1993:159). I have argued earlier that because languages are socially and culturally bound, their effective study requires a positive disposition towards everything the L2 is associated with: its culture, its speakers, its influence. In addition, an appropriate and perceptive spirit also involves an open-minded, cosmopolitan interest in foreign languages and in 'foreignness' in general. The term 'integrativeness' has been used to conveniently cover all these complex attitudes and interests.

Further reading on teaching culture

Summarising all the strategies that have been developed to teach 'culture', that is, to help to break down the cross-cultural barriers in the learners and to prepare them for competent intercultural communication, is beyond the scope of this book. A good theoretical summary has been provided by a recent book – *Language Learners as Ethnographers* – written by some of the best-known British experts in the field (Roberts, Byram, Barro, Jordan and Street 2001). A large variety of practical ideas can be found in activity books such as Tomalin and Stempleski (1993) and Seelye (1993). For more discussion, see for example Byram (1997), Kramsch (1998) and Lustig and Koester (1999).

Promoting integrative values and a cosmopolitan outlook has received a lot of attention recently, partly because of the seeming inability of members of different cultures to communicate harmoniously with each other. Some scholars claim that the main goal of language teaching should not be simply to teach communicative competence but rather 'intercultural communicative competence' (cf. Byram 1997). Indeed, we can find more and more language programmes worldwide with an integrated 'culture' component. The importance of this value dimension also suggests that the traditional practice of teaching languages through their cultures and the social reality of their speakers does have a sound theoretical basis. Without intending to be comprehensive (see the

Further Reading box), let me list a few approaches that can be used to make the L2 'real', to promote integrative values and to raise cross-cultural awareness:

- Familiarise learners with interesting/relevant aspects of the L2 culture.
- Develop learners' cross-cultural awareness systematically by focusing on cross-cultural similarities (and not just differences) and by using analogies to make the strange familiar.
- Collect common stereotypes and prejudices about the L2 speakers and discuss how valid these are.
- Share your own positive L2-related experiences in class.
- Collect quotations and statements by well-known public figures about the significance of language learning and share these with your students.
- Bring various cultural products (e.g. magazines, music, TV recordings, videos) to class.
- Supplement the coursebook with authentic materials (if you have some).
- Encourage learners to discover interesting information about the country/countries where the L2 is spoken on the internet (if they have access to it) and to prepare a presentation.
- Arrange meetings with L2 speakers and invite some interesting native-speaking guests to class.
- Organise school trips or exchange programmes to the L2 community.
- Find L2 speaking pen-friends (or 'keyboard-friends') for your students and draw their attention to internet 'chat rooms' (if they can have access to these).

Strategy 11

Promote 'integrative' values by encouraging a positive and open-minded disposition towards the L2 and its speakers, and towards foreignness in general.

More specifically:

- Include a sociocultural component in your language curriculum.
- Quote positive views about language learning by influential public figures.
- Encourage learners to conduct their own exploration of the L2 community (e.g. on the internet).
- Promote contact with L2 speakers and L2 cultural products.

Instrumental values

Instrumental values are related to the perceived practical, pragmatic benefits that the mastery of the L2 might bring about such as:

- earning extra money;
- getting a promotion;
- pursuing further studies where the L2 is a requirement;
- improving one's social position;
- pursuing hobbies and other leisure activities which require the language (e.g. computing), etc.

(In this section I will not talk about other extrinsic motives such as rewards, punishment, grades, prizes and celebration – these will be discussed in detail in Section 5.4.)

Well said . . .

'It is often difficult to motivate these pupils with the fact that one day they may visit the country. *I don't want to go there anyway* is a common retort.'
(Jennifer Alison 1993:11)

In some respect, instrumental strategies offer the simplest method of addressing the value aspect of motivation, because by using them we do not need to change or improve existing values but rather simply link the successful completion of the task to consequences that the students already value (Brophy 1998). The more direct this link is and the more valuable the consequences are, the more effective the strategy is. To create lasting mental associations between L2 proficiency and desirable outcomes you may include, from time to time, discussions about the life application value of knowing an L2. You may also invite former students who have made a career using the L2 to talk about how they use the language.

An alternative way to clearly demonstrate the usefulness of L2 proficiency is to have students apply what they have previously learned in their daily life. Encourage them from an early stage to use (if they have access to) various internet facilities (e.g. discussion groups, e-mail chat rooms) and later to actively seek the company of L2 speakers. You may even suggest that they use their newly learnt language competence for the study of other subject matters, for example by reading/ translating relevant articles.

Strategy 12

Promote the students' awareness of the instrumental values associated with the knowledge of an L2.

More specifically:

- Regularly remind students that the successful mastery of the L2 is instrumental to the accomplishment of their valued goals.
- Reiterate the role the L2 plays in the world, highlighting its potential usefulness both for themselves and their community.
- Encourage the learners to apply their L2 proficiency in real-life situations.

3.2 Increasing the learners' expectancy of success

The notion of 'expectancy of success' has been one of the most researched factors in motivational psychology for the past four decades, which is due to the undeniable fact that we do things best if we believe we can succeed. Similarly, we learn best when we expect success. Of course, expectancy of success is not enough in itself if it is not accompanied by positive values; we are unlikely to initiate a task, even if we expect to succeed in it, that we do not enjoy and that does not lead to valued outcomes. Expectancy of success and values go hand in hand, which is why motivation theories that are based on these two key components are called 'expectancy-value theories' (see Section 1.1).

Well said . . .

'The simplest way to ensure that students expect success is to make sure that they achieve it consistently . . .'
(Jere Brophy 1998:60)

Whether or not a student will expect success in a given task is a subjective matter, often not very closely related to objective external estimates. On the analogy of the saying, 'Beauty is in the eyes of the beholder' we can state that 'Expectancy is in the mind of the learner'. Therefore, a potentially fruitful area of motivating learners is to increase their expectancies by consciously arranging the conditions in a way that they put the learner in a more positive or optimistic mood. Besides the obvious prerequisite that we should not give learners tasks that are too difficult for them, there are several other methods for achieving heightened success expectations:

- *Provide sufficient preparation.* The perceived likelihood of success does not depend only on how difficult the task is but also on how well the learners are prepared for the task. Pre-task activities have become standard features in modern language teaching methodologies, and these tasks increase success potential. Well-selected strategies and procedures recommended by the teacher fulfil the same role. (See more on how to present tasks in a motivating manner in Section 4.2.)
- *Offer assistance.* If the students know that they can count on your ongoing guidance and help while they are engaged in a learning activity, this knowledge will naturally increase their expectation of success. A task that would be too difficult for students left to their own devices might be just right when carried out with your support (Brophy 1998).
- *Let students help each other.* One reason why cooperative, small group tasks are particularly motivating is that students know that they also have their peers working towards the same goals, resulting in a 'safety in numbers' kind of assurance (Dörnyei 1997).
- *Make the success criteria as clear as possible.* Students can only expect to be successful with confidence if it is quite clear what 'success' means in the particular context. The criteria for success need to be obvious to them from the beginning of learning if they are to know which elements of their performance and production are essential. When the criteria are public and clear, students have a 'road map' to success and can self-evaluate their learning as they proceed (Wlodkowski 1986). If the success criteria involve assessment of the students' achievement (as is often the case), it is useful for them to know the exact format of the tests (i.e. length, type of questions/ items), the specific content areas that will be covered and the evaluation criteria. Past tests and papers can give realistic examples of what is to be expected.
- *Model success.* Even if the success criteria have been well specified, there may be some learners who simply cannot imagine what preparing for these will involve and therefore keep wondering if they can cope. They will find it very useful to see some 'live demonstration', that is, examples of students successfully performing the expected learning activity. This modelling task can be effectively done by peers or past students, but video recordings can also be success-

fully used for the purpose of demonstrating what learners are expected to achieve.

- *Consider and remove potential obstacles to learning.* Wlodkowski (1986) highlights the fact that when students face a learning sequence (whether a specific task or a longer stretch) many will inevitably start thinking about what might interfere with the attainment of the goal. Such intruding factors might be varied in nature: a lack of enough time; other obligations; insufficient resources; disturbance by others, etc. It enhances the learners' expectancy of success if you address these issues in advance, possibly by involving the learners themselves. Even if you cannot offer any immediate solutions, the fact that the students have been reminded of these potential obstructions will give them more time to plan ahead.

Strategy 13

Increase the students' expectancy of success in particular tasks and in learning in general.

More specifically:

- Make sure that they receive sufficient preparation and assistance.
- Make sure they know exactly what success in the task involves.
- Make sure that there are no serious obstacles to success.

3.3 Increasing the learners' goal-orientedness

Educational authorities in many parts of the world are getting into the habit of requiring teachers to specify their teaching goals with an ever-increasing elaborateness. Many of us are often required to spend long hours preparing sizeable documents detailing the general aims and objectives of each course we teach (based on the centrally distributed curricular guidelines), and the specific teaching purpose of each session within these courses (following the official syllabus specifications). However, these goal descriptions are often quite distinct from the goals the students are actually pursuing during those same classes. In fact, research has repeatedly found that in an ordinary class many if not most students do not really understand (or accept) why they are involved in a learning activity. The 'official class goal' (i.e. mastering the course content) may well not be the class group's only goal and in some cases may not be a group goal at all!

Well said . . .

'It is fundamental to the successful working of a group to have a sense of direction and a common purpose. Defining and agreeing aims is one of the hardest tasks that the group has to undertake together.'
(Jill Hadfield 1992:134)

This potential goal diversity became obvious to me during one of the first adult evening L2 courses I had ever taught. This course was in many ways a most inspiring and successful experience: the group bonded well, the group spirit soared high, there was hardly any student attrition, and we generally had a good time. There was only one 'slight' problem: with the growing maturity of the group there was less and less actual learning taking place in the class. I spent long hours with a psychologist friend, who was at the same time a learner in this group, trying to figure out what was going on. The answer we eventually came up with was that some time during the course of the programme the group shifted its main goal: because personal relations within the group were becoming so very rewarding, social rather than academic goals became the group's main concern. To be fair, this made perfect sense from their point of view; after all, in considering the members' general well-being, to belong to an accepting and supportive community and to acquire a group of new friends is just as important as mastering the English language.

Well said . . .

'Although researchers are not agreed on the precise relationship between individual and group goals, there is general consensus that if any small group is to develop into a mature work group capable of functioning productively, all group members must share the same group goal. Ostensibly, this would not appear to be a problem for English language classes, because in theory all class members have the same goal: the development of proficiency in English. In practice the situation is very different, and language teachers . . . may well need to spend some time establishing broad group goals.'
(Rosemary Senior 1997:5)

My experience of this is not confined to adult education. We must realise that for the average school pupils the 'school' represents primarily a social arena and not the scene of academic work. They are there because they have to rather than because they want to perform tasks, and they are often more interested in issues such as love, personal image or social standing than the mastery of school subjects. In fact, recent research on school motivation has emphasised that the only way to really understand what is going on at the motivational level of classrooms is by looking at the interplay of academic and social motives (cf. Juvonen and Wentzel 1996; Wentzel 1999). What all this implies is that at any given time when you want your students to focus on certain goals you may find some of them pursue other goals in addition or instead. How can we handle this inherent goal diversity? Can the class group's goal-orientedness be consciously increased?

A certain amount of goal conflict and goal ambiguity will, I am afraid, always characterise a class of, say, 30 lively teenagers, but well selected goal-setting strategies can be surprisingly successful in getting learners on task. The most obvious strategy is to initiate a discussion with the students about goals in general. I have found that when participants on a new language course were asked to share openly their *own* personal goals, this usually revealed considerable differences, which in turn led to a fruitful negotiation process with the objective of outlining 'class goals'. You have won half the motivation battle if the class group can agree on a common purpose and sense of direction by taking into account:

- *individual goals* (which may range from having fun to passing the exam or to getting the minimum grade level required for survival);
- *institutional constraints* ('you're here to learn the L2; this is the syllabus for this year');
- *success criteria* (which traditionally have had to do with exams and marks, but other communicative criteria can often be a better incentive, e.g. to be able to understand most of the lyrics of a pop group, or other specific communicative objectives).

The composite group goal can then be displayed on a wall chart. It is important to also mention that the initial effort to establish a 'class goal' will need to be followed up by a recurring review of the original goal(s) in view of the progress made towards them. Such 'goal reviews' can give both the teacher and the learner a chance to evaluate and regain momentum.

> *How do goals affect performance?*
>
> There are four mechanisms by which goals affect the students' performance:
>
> - They direct attention and effort towards goal-relevant activities at the expense of irrelevant or distracting actions.
> - They regulate the amount of effort people expend in that people adjust their effort to the difficulty level required by the task.
> - They encourage persistence until the goal is accomplished.
> - They promote the search for relevant action plans or task strategies.

Finally, because of the inherent interaction of academic and social goals in the classroom, the most motivating activities and experiences for the students are likely to be those that involve the simultaneous pursuit and attainment of both types of goals (Ford 1992). I will come back to this question in Section 4.5 when I discuss the importance of allowing learners to maintain a positive social image in class. Also, there will be more on goals in Section 4.3, which will concentrate on short-term goal-setting procedures.

Strategy 14

Increase your students' goal-orientedness by formulating explicit class goals accepted by them.

More specifically:

- Have the students negotiate their individual goals and outline a common purpose, and display the final outcome in public.
- Draw attention from time to time to the class goals and how particular activities help to attain them.
- Keep the class goals achievable by re-negotiating if necessary.

3.4 Making the teaching materials relevant for the learners

The core of the issue that this section addresses has been very succinctly summarised by McCombs and Whisler (1997:38): 'Educators think students do not care, while the students tell us they do care about learning but are not getting what they need.' Indeed, one of the most demotivating factors for learners is when they have to learn something that they cannot see the point of because it has no seeming relevance whatsoever to their lives. This experience is unfortunately more common than many of us would think. After all, as Brophy (1998) argues, most schools' curricular topics and learning activities are selected primarily on the basis of what society believes students need to learn, not on the basis of what students would choose if given the opportunity to do so. 'Schools are established for the benefits of students, but from the students' point of view their time in the classroom is devoted to enforced attempts to meet externally imposed demands' (p. 10). Accordingly, much of the motivational advice offered to teachers in the educational literature boils down to the following general principle: *Find out what your students' goals are and what topics they want to learn about, then build these into your curriculum as much as possible.* This makes sense: students will not be motivated to learn unless they regard the material they are taught as worth learning.

Well said . . .

'If the teacher is to motivate pupils to learn, then relevance has to be the red thread permeating activities. If pupils fail to see the relationship between the activity and the world in which they live, then the point of the activity is likely to be lost on them. . . . If pupils do not see the relevance of a subject, the teacher has from the outset a major challenge.'
(Gary Chambers 1999:37–8)

The other side of the coin is that in countries where there is a special emphasis on achievement standards in school, there is increased pressure on teachers to prepare their learners to take language exams as fast as possible. Many teachers respond to this pressure by narrowing the curriculum and teaching to the test. Given that the vast majority of language exams and tests fail to assess real communicative language content, teaching communicative skills becomes/remains a neglected component in many L2 classrooms regardless of the unquestionable fact that most learners learn an L2 with the purpose of being able to communicate in it. This problem of not meeting students' needs is further augmented by the constant time pressure most teachers work under. There is simply not enough time for most of us to personalise the curriculum, to elaborate on certain points and to supplement the material where necessary.

So, for various reasons we are pretty much stuck with the ready-made curriculum, which is usually a coursebook. I don't know what you think of the books you are using but my impression is that even the best ones are often like leisure magazines in that they are full of colourful and 'interesting' bits which somehow fail to reach the person who reads them. In order to make these texts motivating, we need to relate the subjects to the everyday experiences and backgrounds of the students. To do so, I have often used in my teaching an activity type which I called 'How would it go at home?'. In this, students are asked to imagine how a particular theme from the coursebook could be transferred to locations and situations associated with their own life experiences. Such tasks can be a lot of fun as they often highlight interesting contrasts, produce unintentional or intentional parodies and, in general, add a personal touch. In multi-ethnic learner groups such activities can also contribute to cross-cultural awareness raising.

word 'sex' in a coursebook I was writing (the compromise we achieved in the end was that I was allowed to write about 'contraception'. . .). Some time later a friend of mine received back a manuscript from his editor with one of the best units crossed out, saying 'Excellent idea; use it elsewhere . . .'.

Let us suppose for a moment that we are not totally tied up by institutional and curricular constraints and that we have a certain amount of leeway to liven up the course material. What can we do to make the teaching materials relevant to the learners in such an 'ideal' world?

The first step has to involve our *finding out* about the interests, hobbies and needs of our learners: If we wish to relate content to student interests and experiences, we need to be knowledgeable about them. This can be done by means of:

- *interviews* and *one-to-one chats*;
- *group discussion* and *brainstorming* (e.g. about events or people that the students find significant; places they would like to go to; life styles they envy or disapprove of, etc.);
- *essay writing assignments*;
- *questionnaires with open-ended questions* (e.g. 'If you didn't have to come to school tomorrow, what would you like to do most?' or 'What are your main concerns about how people live in . . .?' or even 'What would you like to get out of these classes most?');
- *questionnaires with sentence-completion items* (e.g. learners are asked to finish the following sentence beginnings: 'Something I want to do more often is . . .', 'I am afraid of . . .', 'I think people should . . .').

Needs analyses of this sort usually provide a rich set of data, which can then be submitted to further discussion and fine-tuning. A class in which the basic motivational conditions are in place (cf. Chapter 2) should be able to arrive at a set of truly meaningful items representing the members' interest, fantasies and ideals.

Jennifer Alison (1993) mentions a further important point about teaching teenagers when she emphasises that we should find a course content which is sufficiently 'adult', that is, that can bring the youngsters into contact with the adult world.

In terms of the students' language needs you may want to focus/build on:

- what (if any) L2-related activities they are currently involved in (e.g. computer games);

- what L2 contacts they have (if any);
- which L2 skills they consider most important/useful;
- what L2-related goals they have (if any);
- what they can imagine using the L2 for if they could speak it;
- what L2-related situations they can visualise themselves in one day.

When you are ready for the second stage of the process, that is, to use the obtained information to *link* classroom topics and activities to the students' real life experiences and preferences, there is no reason why you couldn't enlist the help of the students themselves. They are bound to be interested in planning their own course programme and discussing the choice of the teaching materials (both textbooks and supplementary materials). Many of them would also enjoy writing 'alternative units' for a coursebook, or designing thematic presentations or games. Furthermore, Wlodkowski (1986) suggests that reporting back the information obtained through the needs analysis phase to the learners might demonstrate to them how the resultant course objectives and content reflect their views, which is motivating in itself.

Strategy 15

Make the curriculum and the teaching materials relevant to the students.

More specifically:

- Use needs analysis techniques to find out about your students' needs, goals and interests, and then build these into your curriculum as much as possible.
- Relate the subject matter to the everyday experiences and backgrounds of the students.
- Enlist the students in designing and running the course.

3.5 Creating realistic learner beliefs

Most learners will have certain beliefs about language learning and most of these beliefs are likely to be (at least partly) incorrect. Some may think that you can master a language in a few months, and others might believe that even years of suffering may not be sufficient. Some may think that you can only learn the L2 in the host environment, and others might believe that L2 learning in school contexts can be useful if a child starts early enough. Some may think that starting 'early' should mean about 8 or 9 years old, and others might believe that anything over 5 is already too late. Some may think that you need a special 'knack' for languages to be able to learn them, and others might believe that hard work and persistence should be enough. Some may think that grammatical errors are to be avoided at all cost, and others might believe that mistakes do not matter as long as one is fluent. The list is endless.

Of course, issues like the above are not unambiguous and even language experts have disagreements. Fortunately, applied linguistics has (more or less) reached a state of maturity where some of the most extreme views can be refuted with confidence (see 'Further reading on how languages are learnt' in the box below). I believe that it is important that we do so because incorrect beliefs can become real barriers to the mastery of an L2. Unrealistic beliefs about how much progress to expect and how fast, can function like 'time bombs' at the beginning of a language course because of the inevitable disappointment that is to follow. Rigid convictions about what is important about a language and what's not, or what's the best way of learning, can clash with your teaching approach, thereby hindering progress. The best thing is to sort out some of the most far-fetched expectations and erroneous assumptions early on in the course.

Further reading on how languages are learnt

Much further research is needed before we can provide a detailed account of how second languages are learnt and how various factors affect the process. Nevertheless, during the past few years several concise and accessible summaries have been published with a view to the language practitioner. Lightbown and Spada (1999) offer a readable introduction to first and second language acquisition and up-to-date reference material has been offered by three recent encyclopaedias (Byram 2000; Corson 1997; Spolsky 1999). Interestingly three other publishers are also coming out with edited volumes that survey the broad spectrum of L2 studies from the language teacher's perspective in the near future (Carter and Nunan 2001; Schmitt in press; Kaplan in press).

What is the best way of confronting false learner beliefs? My suggestion is that you should definitely talk about some of the key issues with the students, perhaps in the form of a negotiated pyramid discussion (see

Section 2.3 for a description of how this works). The main points to be addressed could involve the following:

- The difficulty of language learning in general and learning the specific L2 they are studying in particular.
- The realistic rate of progress students can expect.
- What is required from the learner to be successful.
- How languages are best learned.

Regarding the third point, it is important to emphasise the need of *effort* without portraying it as some tedious chore but more as an *investment* (Brophy 1998). I have also found it useful to point out that the majority of the people in the world *are* bilingual, and many of these learnt their second language later in life – which indicates that a lack of aptitude can be compensated for by persistence and careful work. Also, many adults may believe that they are too old to begin new learning activities – an assumption that is best refuted by citing examples of successful adult language learners.

With regard to the last point – i.e. how languages are best learnt – I think it is very important to emphasise that at the moment we do not know of a 'perfect' method for learning foreign languages; the mastery of an L2 can be achieved in a number of different ways, using diverse strategies, and therefore a key factor in achieving success is for learners to discover for themselves the methods and techniques by which they learn best.

An effective way of initiating discussions is to administer to the students a short questionnaire on learner beliefs developed by Elaine Horwitz (1988) and use the answers as a starting point in analysing the validity of popular beliefs and myths. Horwitz's 'Beliefs About Language Learning Inventory' (BALLI) consists of 34 items to assess student beliefs in five major areas: difficulty of language learning, foreign language aptitude, the nature of language learning, learning and communication strategies, and motivation and expectations (for the actual items, see the box below).

Elaine Horwitz's Beliefs About Language Learning Inventory (BALLI)

(The items have been grouped according to their themes; in the original they were presented mixed up. Unless otherwise instructed, respondents indicate the degree of their agreement with these statements by marking one of five response options: 1 = strongly agree; 2 = agree; 3 = neither agree nor disagree; 4 = disagree; 5 = strongly disagree.)

THE DIFFICULTY OF LANGUAGE LEARNING

- Some languages are easier to learn than others.
- The language I am trying to learn is: 1) a very difficult language, 2) a difficult language, 3) a language of medium difficulty, 4) an easy language, 5) a very easy language.
- I believe that I will ultimately learn to speak this language very well.
- If someone spent one hour a day learning this language, how long would it take him/her to become fluent? 1) less than a year, 2) 1–2 years, 3) 3–5 years, 4) 5–10 years, 5) You can't learn a language in 1 hour a day.
- It is easier to speak than to understand a foreign language.
- It is easier to read and write this language than to speak and understand it.

FOREIGN LANGUAGE APTITUDE

- It is easier for children than adults to learn a foreign language.
- Some people are born with a special ability which helps them to learn a foreign language.
- It is easier for someone who already speaks a foreign language to learn another one.
- I have foreign language aptitude.
- Women are better than men at learning foreign languages.
- People who are good at maths and science are not good at learning foreign languages.
- People who speak more than one language well are very intelligent.
- Americans are good at learning foreign languages.
- Everyone can learn to speak a foreign language.

THE NATURE OF LANGUAGE LEARNING

- It is necessary to know the foreign culture in order to speak the foreign language.
- It is better to learn the foreign language in the foreign country.
- Learning the foreign language is mostly a matter of learning a lot of new vocabulary words.
- Learning the foreign language is mostly a matter of learning a lot of grammar rules.
- Learning a foreign language is different from learning other school subjects.

- Learning a foreign language is mostly a matter of translating from English.

LEARNING AND COMMUNICATION STRATEGIES

- It is important to repeat and practise a lot.
- It is important to practise in the language laboratory.
- It is important to speak a foreign language with an excellent accent.
- You shouldn't say anything in the foreign language until you can say it correctly.
- If I heard someone speaking the language I am trying to learn, I would go up to them so that I could practise speaking the language.
- It's o.k. to guess if you don't know a word in the foreign language.
- I feel self-conscious speaking the foreign language in front of other people.
- If you are allowed to make mistakes in the beginning it will be hard to get rid of them later on.

MOTIVATION AND EXPECTATIONS

- If I get to speak this language very well, I will have many opportunities to use it.
- If I learn to speak this language very well, it will help me get a good job.
- Americans think that it is important to speak a foreign language.
- I would like to learn this language so that I can get to know its speakers better.

(Elaine Horwitz 1988; used with permission)

Strategy 16

Help to create realistic learner beliefs.

More specifically:

- Positively confront the possible erroneous beliefs, expectations, and assumptions that learners may have.
- Raise the learners' general awareness about the different ways languages are learnt and the number of factors that can contribute to success.

4 Maintaining and protecting motivation

Let us suppose that all the ingredients for generating a motivating classroom environment are in place and our students approach the learning situation with positive L2-related values, high expectancy of success, sufficient goal clarity, a general interest in the teaching material on offer and realistic beliefs. Have we successfully completed our motivational agenda? Not quite. If you refer back to the process model of motivation in Section 1.1 (Figure 2), you can see that one aspect of the model is particularly prominent: the *actional stage*. I argued there that it is one thing to initially whet the students' appetite with appropriate motivational techniques, but when action has commenced and is well on the way, a set of new motivational influences (some negative and some positive) come into force, and unless motivation is actively maintained and protected during this phase, the natural tendency to lose sight of the goal, to get tired or bored of the activity and to give way to attractive distractions will result in the initial motivation gradually petering out. In short, motivation needs to be actively nurtured.

Well said . . .

'*Any learning activity can become satiating*; it happens to everyone, often without any intention on our part. Satiation is what lies behind the "divine discontent" of human existence.'
(Raymond Wlodkowski 1986:144)

Happily, the spectrum of motivation maintenance (or 'executive motivational') strategies is particularly rich, since ongoing human behaviour can be modified in so many different ways, ranging from the manner we present and administer tasks to teaching the learners how to motivate themselves. This chapter will survey the eight most powerful executive motivational areas.

4.1 Making learning stimulating and enjoyable

People are usually quite willing to spend a great deal of time thinking and learning while pursuing activities they *enjoy*. Just think of all the hours we devote to, say, doing crosswords, rehearsing for amateur theatre performances or fiddling with the computer. These examples suggest that learning does not necessarily have to be a boring and tedious chore (which it very often is). If we could somehow make the learning process more stimulating and enjoyable, that would greatly contribute to sustained learner involvement. This is an assumption that most motivational psychologists subscribe to and which also makes a lot of sense to classroom teachers – indeed, many practitioners would simply equate the adjective 'motivating' with 'interesting'.

Can you still remember?

'When I was a teenager – you know what I mean, that's always a problem for everybody – when I was a teenager, as I said, I would prefer to be with my friends or to be at home watching TV. Sometimes I was in the class and I was looking at the clock saying, "Oh, please let it run faster!" and sometimes the teacher was talking and I was not listening because I was really anxious to go out and be somewhere else, you know?'
(From an interview with a learner of English; adapted from Silva 2001)

Let us start with a puzzling question. If both theoreticians and practitioners agree on the importance of making learning stimulating and enjoyable, why does available research indicate that the general characteristic of classroom learning is usually just the opposite: unglamorous and drudgery-like? Well, there are several reasons:

- Many teachers (and also students) share the belief that serious learning is supposed to be hard work, and if it is enjoyable, it is doubtful that it is serious or significant. Indeed, as Raffini (1996:11) summarises well, 'too often the word "enjoyable" has a bad reputation in school'.
- With increasing pressures on teachers to cover the curriculum and to prepare students for tests and exams, their emphasis inevitably shifts from the process – the extent of learner involvement and enjoyment – to the product, that is, to producing fast and tangible outcomes.
- Not all assignments can be fully engaging. We have to teach the whole curriculum and certain parts are bound to be less attractive for

the students than others. Covington and Teel (1996:90) rightly point out that we teachers are not in the entertainment business, and cannot be expected to turn everything into fun.

- School learning includes a lot of seatwork. This is in spite of the fact that, as already mentioned, most school learners are in the most active phase of their physical development and find it extremely difficult to spend most of the working day practically motionless.

This has been the bad news. The good news is that there is an impressive array of motivational strategies that have been found to be effective in livening up classroom learning. This suggests that, within what is feasible, we might be able to find an angle for making learning more stimulating in many, if not most, situations. Broadly speaking, we can pursue three main types of strategy:

- *breaking the monotony of learning,*
- *making the tasks more interesting,*
- *increasing the involvement of the students.*

Of course, these three stimulation goals overlap. What breaks the monotony of learning will also make the process more interesting, and what is interesting may encourage further student involvement. Yet I find that it makes the discussion clearer if we address these issues independently. We should also note here that all the other motivational aspects discussed later in this chapter also contribute to the quality of the learning experience, since in a way everything that motivates students to learn increases the attraction of the course.

Well said . . .

'*Ensure success.* . . . We can bend over backwards explaining the advantages of speaking a foreign language but the pupils' outlook is often more immediate than that. They like what they are good at.'
(Jenifer Alison 1993:12)

Breaking the monotony of learning

Even in classes characterised by a mixture of interesting teaching approaches, there is a danger that as the school year progresses, both teachers and students can easily settle into familiar routines. The routines, then, can easily turn into a monotonous 'daily grind', with the class losing its 'edge'. Monotony is inversely related to variety. In order to break monotony, we need to vary as many aspects of the learning process as possible. First and foremost are the *language tasks*. For example, we can vary the:

- linguistic focus of the tasks (e.g. a grammar task can be followed by one focusing on sociocultural issues);
- main language skills the tasks activate (e.g. a writing task can be followed by a speaking activity);
- channel of communication (varying auditory, visual and tactile modes of dealing with learning; selectively using visual aids);
- organisational format (e.g. a whole-class task can be followed by group work or pair work).

Variety, however, is not confined to tasks alone. It can also concern other aspects of the teaching/learning process, such as:

- our presentation style;
- the learning materials;
- the extent of student involvement (e.g. occasionally students lead some of the activities);
- the classroom's spatial organisation (e.g. how the tables and chairs are arranged).

The final aspect of how to break the monotony of classroom teaching concerns the *general rhythm and sequence of events*. Although various teaching events in a class are traditionally based on the 'logical flow of information' (Wlodkowski 1986:145), from a motivational perspective the 'motivational flow' is just as important. For example, it may be worth starting the class with a *'warmer'*, which can be a short, stimulating game, to set the tone. Or, a slow section of the lesson that requires contemplation can be followed by a break involving some sort of movement, or a fast sequence of events requiring a different kind of concentration (e.g. a short game).

Of course, I am not trying to suggest that instructors should systematically and continuously vary all the above aspects of their teaching – that would be the perfect recipe for teacher burn-out. Rather, we may look at these variables as, say, cooking ingredients, and all we need to make sure is that we don't serve exactly the same meal every day. And, to top it off, we may want, from time to time, to *do the unexpected*. An occasional departure from what the students have come to expect can cause the final surge in the motivational flow (what a metaphor . . .).

Strategy 17

Make learning more stimulating and enjoyable by breaking the monotony of classroom events.

More specifically:

- Vary the learning tasks and other aspects of your teaching as much as you can.
- Focus on the motivational flow and not just the information flow in your class.
- Occasionally do the unexpected.

Making the tasks more interesting

Varying the tasks is important but not even the richest variety will motivate if the content of the tasks is not attractive to the students – that is, if the task is *boring*. The literature contains an abundance of suggestions on how to make tasks interesting. The trouble is that in real life most of the tasks we use are prescribed by the official course syllabus or coursebook, and teachers usually have little time to introduce new activities. So, when I list the most commonly quoted characteristics of motivating tasks, it is in the hope that some of these might just lend themselves to modifying some official task.

What's wrong with boredom?

Humans are, in fact, amazingly capable of producing concentrated effort when they want to, regardless of any uninspiring presentation or dull practice sequence (self-motivating strategies, as discussed in Section 4.8, come in very handy at times like these). The real problem with boredom is twofold:

- It is a fertile ground for disruptions – sometimes we can hardly wait for an excuse to 'take a break'.
- It does not inspire further, continuing motivation. Boring but systematic teaching can be effective in getting short-term results, but rarely does it inspire a life-long commitment to the subject matter.

What are the most motivating features of task content? Here are some ideas:

- *Challenge*: Humans like to be challenged, as evidenced by our continual fascination with crosswords, puzzles or computer games, and the same applies to taking risks if those are moderate. This means that tasks in which learners need to solve problems, discover something, overcome obstacles, avoid traps, find hidden information, etc. are always welcome.

- *Interesting content*: A simple but effective way to raise task interest is to connect the topic with things that students already find interesting or hold in esteem. For example, including prominent events or people from the youth culture can add an attractive dimension to the activity. Learning about, say, daily routines can become much more interesting by focusing on a famous pop star, trying to imagine what he/she does and does not do.

- *The novelty element*: If something about the activity is new or different or unfamiliar or totally unexpected, this will certainly help to eliminate boredom.

- *The intriguing element*: Tasks which concern ambiguous, problematic, paradoxical, controversial, contradictory or incongruous material stimulate curiosity by creating a conceptual conflict that needs to be resolved.

- *The exotic element*: We all like learning about places and people which are unique and have a certain amount of grandeur.

- *The fantasy element*: Tasks are inherently captivating if they engage the learner's fantasy. Everybody, children and adults alike, enjoy using their imagination for creating make-believe stories, identifying with fictional characters or acting out pretend play.

- *The personal element*: There is something inherently interesting about learning about the everyday life of real people (I don't know why); this has been capitalised on by TV soap operas and their generally high viewing rates prove that the principle works. In a similar vein, many stilted coursebook tasks can be made stimulating by personalising them, that is, by relating the content to the learners' own lives.

Well said . . .

'If we consider the students in our classes to be more interesting than the rather cardboard characters found in the traditional coursebook, it follows that a real need exists for activities where the students are invited to speak to each other and express their ideas using structures that have already been presented to them. Practising structures in this very personal series of contexts is much more emotionally real than practising them in the make-belief world of a textbook.'
(Frank and Rinvolucri 1991:6)

- *Competition*: The opportunity to compete can add excitement to learning tasks, regardless of whether the competition is for prizes (e.g. a packet of sweets) or merely for the satisfaction of winning. The only problem with small group competition is, as Brophy (1998) emphasises, that you cannot have winners without losers, and the latter usually outnumber the former. Make sure, therefore, that losers do not take it very seriously . . .
- *Tangible outcome*: Tasks which require learners to create some kind of a finished product as the outcome (e.g. student newsletter, a poster, a radio programme, an information brochure or a piece of artwork) can engage students to an unprecedented extent.
- *Humour*: 'Humour is many things and one of them is interesting' (Wlodkowski 1986:161).

Strategy 18

Make learning stimulating and enjoyable for the learner by increasing the attractiveness of the tasks.

More specifically:

- Make tasks challenging.
- Make task content attractive by adapting it to the students' natural interests or by including novel, intriguing, exotic, humorous, competitive or fantasy elements.
- Personalise learning tasks.
- Select tasks that yield tangible, finished products.

Increasing student involvement

People usually enjoy a task if they play an essential part in it. This is well illustrated by class discussions, which are usually perceived to be interesting by those who have contributed to it and boring by those who have not. This means that another way of making learning stimulating and enjoyable is creating learning situations where learners are required to become active participants. Sometimes learners need a more direct nudge than merely presenting an opportunity for participation, and handing out specific roles (e.g. on cards) or giving them personalised assignments are necessary to provide the needed momentum.

> ### Strategy 19
>
> *Make learning stimulating and enjoyable for the learners by enlisting them as active task participants.*
>
> More specifically:
>
> - Select tasks which require mental and/or bodily involvement from each participant.
> - Create specific roles and personalised assignments for everybody.

4.2 Presenting tasks in a motivating way

Sometimes it is easier said than done that we should make learning stimulating and enjoyable. How often have you managed to teach, for example, the grammatical rules governing the use of the definite article in an 'adventurous' and 'exotic' way, capitalising on the 'arousal value of suspense', while raising the learners' 'epistemic curiosity' and stimulating their 'fantasy' (as recommended in the literature)? The fact is that some topics we teach are unlikely to interest students even though it is in their interest to learn them. This is when motivational techniques related to how to *present* and *administer* tasks come in particularly useful. I have found that the way we present tasks can make a huge difference in how students perceive and approach them. With a proper introduction, even a grammatical substitution drill can be made (almost) exciting. So, what is a 'proper' introduction in the motivational sense?

Beside the traditional purpose of task instructions – namely, to describe what students will be doing, what they will have accomplished when they are finished, and how these accomplishments will be evaluated – the motivational introduction of an activity fulfils at least three further functions:

- It explains the purpose and the utility of the task.
- It whets the students' anticipation of the task.
- It provides appropriate strategies for doing the task.

Interesting research . . .

Jere Brophy (1998:187–8) describes a research project in which he and his colleagues observed how experienced, better-than-average teachers administered tasks in mathematics and reading classes. The disappointing result of the study was that only about a third of the teachers' task introductions included comments which were judged by the researchers as ones that were likely to have positive effects on student motivation. Furthermore, even these comments were mostly only brief predictions that the students would enjoy the task or would do well on it. All in all, in about 100 hours of classroom observation, only nine task introductions were noted that included substantive information related to the motivation to learn!

Explaining the purpose and the utility of a task

Even experienced teachers sometimes expect students to carry out a task without offering them any real explanation about the purpose of the activity. Students are too often required to do things in the classroom just because the teacher says so. In this sense schools (unfortunately) resemble the armed forces, which is not exactly the ideal model for a motivationally conscious teacher. In civilian contexts, the usual way of asking people to do something involves communicating good reasons to them as to why the particular activity is meaningful or important, and I can't see why the introduction of learning tasks should not follow this pattern. If we want our students to give their best when attending to a task, they need to see the point in what they do. As Scheidecker and Freeman (1999:140) summarise:

> Every new unit, every venue of instruction, should be preceded by a justification of its presence. . . . Informed clients are much more likely to join the successful completion of the project voluntarily than disenfranchised students who have been asked to trust the system.

In accordance, it may be useful to cover the following points when presenting a task:

- Emphasise that the task is a learning opportunity to be valued rather than an imposed demand to be resisted.
- Explain where the activity fits in within a sequence or bigger picture, and how it relates to the overall goals of the class.

- Describe the intended purpose of the activity and what this implies about how students should respond to it (e.g. what they should concentrate on or be particularly careful about).
- Try and make a connection between the task and the students' personal daily life, and point out how the skills learnt will be useful in enabling them to achieve real-life agendas.

Whetting the students' appetite

Good task introductions raise the students' expectations of something interesting and important to come. You can do this by:

- projecting intensity and enthusiasm when you introduce the activity; and communicating your expectation for students to succeed;
- asking students to make guesses and predictions about the upcoming activity (e.g. what is going to be covered; how long a listening passage will take, etc.);
- pointing out challenging or important aspects of the L2 content to be learned;
- adding a twist to routine activities (e.g. asking them to do a grammar drill very fast or whispering).

Providing appropriate strategies to do the task

The final aspect of a good task introduction concerns the strategies that students should apply to complete the task successfully. I have often found in the past that when I presented what I considered a very creative communicative activity, some of the learners simply did not concentrate enough on my instructions to understand what was required of them, and others did not really know how to go about completing the task. This was, in a way, understandable: when preparing for the class I spent a relatively long time imagining the activity sequence and envisaging who does what, whereas the students were asked to do all this promptly after the instructions. Therefore, it usually pays off to spend a bit longer demonstrating the task and illustrating some of the strategies that might be particularly effective during task completion as it can effectively sort out any confusion or lingering doubts. I have also developed a very practical rule of thumb for myself: the task instruction should spell out exactly what students need to do immediately after the instruction is over.

Quite so!

'*Work with the learner at the beginning of difficult tasks.* It's amazing what can be lifted and moved with just a little help. Sometimes a learner might have a momentary confusion or not know what to do next. Our proximity and minimal assistance can be just enough for the learner to find the right direction, continue involvement, and gain the initial confidence to proceed with learning.'
(Raymond Wlodkowski 1986:92)

The best way to demonstrate the necessary strategies and skills is to *model* them (another rule of thumb of mine is, 'Never explain, demonstrate!'). You can do this, for example, by pretending to be a student and performing various roles, or you can ask volunteers to act out your guidelines. Another, less commonly used way is the 'think-aloud' technique, which involves saying out loud the various steps taken in approaching and dealing with an issue and how performing a complex task can be broken down into smaller steps. It is also useful to remind students of previously learned knowledge or skills that they can make use of during task completion. Before making a bigger assignment, you can also get the whole class to brainstorm lists of strategies for getting the project done.

Strategy 20

Present and administer tasks in a motivating way.

More specifically:

- Explain the purpose and utility of a task.
- Whet the students' appetite about the content of the task.
- Provide appropriate strategies to carry out the task.

4.3 Setting specific learner goals

We have already talked about *goals* in Section 3.3, but there the focus was on the learners' and – more importantly – the class group's general level of goal-orientedness. However, there is more to goals. Here we will address how specific and short-term goals can help the learner to structure the learning process. This is particularly important in learning a subject such as an L2, where even acquiring a minimum working knowledge may take several years. It is simply unreasonable to expect that the ultimate purpose of the learning process – to communicate with L2 speakers or to understand L2 products – will be strong enough during all this time to maintain the original motivational momentum. In such situations specific, short-term goals (often referred to as 'proximal subgoals' in the psychological literature) might provide immediate extra incentives.

At the same time, goals are not only outcomes to shoot for but also standards by which students can evaluate their own performance and which mark their progress. This is the basis of having 'grade exams' or 'graded certificates' (e.g. 'Level 6', 'Grade 8') in many subject areas such as learning to swim or play the piano. Natural subgoals within the L2 learning context are forthcoming tests, exams or competitions, but goal-setting is not restricted to such 'official' events. Personal goals such as reading a chapter of a book every weekend or learning 10 new words every day may energise learning just as well.

Well said . . .

'Goals are crucial for achievement but they are usually given more prominence in athletics and work environments than in academic learning.'
(Kay Alderman 1999: ix)

Because goal-setting dramatically increases productivity, you can safely guess that work psychologists have shown a particular interest in the concept. Indeed, it has been two organisational psychologists, Edwin Locke and Gary Latham (1990), who have elaborated on and formalised goal setting processes into a coherent theory (cf. also Section 1.1). The theory has been widely used in many organisational contexts to improve employee motivation and performance, and it has proved just as relevant to educational contexts. Having said that, my impression is that this powerful strategy has been largely underutilised in language education. Oxford and Shearin's (1994:19) observation confirms this view: 'Goal-setting can have exceptional importance in stimulating L2 learning motivation, and it is therefore shocking that so little time and energy are spent in the L2 classroom on goal-setting.'

Interesting research . . .

One of the most influential studies in drawing attention to the power of goal-setting has been carried out by Albert Bandura and Dale Schunk (1981). Three groups of students participated in a self-directed instructional programme in maths, in which they had to work their way through a series of sets of teaching materials on 'subtractions'. The three groups were given different goals:

- The first group was given a vague and general goal of working 'productively'.
- The second group was given a distant goal of completing all sets of material by the end of the last session.
- The third group pursued a specific, short-term goal of completing one set of material each session.

The researchers expected significant differences in the rate of progress in the three groups, but the results surprised even them: By the end of four sessions, the percentage of the total instructional material completed was 74 per cent in the group with the specific, short-term goal, 55 per cent in the distal goal condition, and 53 per cent in the group which only had a vague, general goal.

The underutilised nature of goal-setting in L2 education is all the more surprising because goal-setting is basically a simple planning process that can be learned relatively easily. The main point is to show students how to break down tasks and assignments into small steps, how to assign deadlines to these, and how to monitor their own progress. McCombs and Pope (1994:68) offer a straightforward template for students with the following seven steps:

1 Define your goal clearly.
2 List steps to take to reach this goal.
3 Think of problems that might come up that would interfere.
4 Think of solutions to these problems.
5 Set a timeline for reaching the goal.
6 Evaluate your progress.
7 Reward yourself for accomplishments.

Jones and Jones (1995) point out that the evaluation phase (Step 6) can even involve teaching students to chart their own improvements on a regular basis.

What are the characteristics of the goals that work best? Based on the work of Pintrich and Schunk (1996) and Dembo and Eaton (1997), I have compiled the following set of principles:

1 Goals should be:
  - *clear* and *specific*, describing concrete outcomes in as much detail as possible;
  - *measurable*, describing the outcome in terms that can be clearly evaluated;
  - *challenging* and *difficult*, but not outside the range of students' capabilities;
  - *realistic*.
2 Goals should have a stated *completion date*.
3 Both *short-term* and *long-term* goals should be set.
4 Teachers should provide *feedback* that increases the students' capability of and confidence in obtaining the goal.

McCombs and Pope (1994:69) recommend teaching students a simple device, the 'ABCD' of goals: A goal should be:

Achievable (reasonable for your age and strengths),
Believable (you need to believe you can accomplish it),
Conceivable (clearly stated and measurable),
Desirable (you really want it, and others want it for you).

Alison (1993) emphasises that goal-setting techniques can also be used effectively with demotivated, reluctant students, who have no general goals whatsoever associated with language learning (i.e. they don't particularly want to communicate with L2 speakers, and can't see any ways in which an L2 would be useful for them in the future). Goal-setting allows teachers to look at the tasks from these learners' point of view and create an immediate purpose that is valid in their eyes. This can be, for example, taking on a challenge, beating the teacher, beating a record, winning a game or creating something concrete for others to use or see.

If you like the idea of goal-setting and are thinking of introducing it in your class, you may want to do it on a regular basis, encouraging students to set weekly or monthly goals. Although quite time-consuming, a regular *goal-setting conference* with each student can provide this process with a firm structure. Alternatively, you may list from time to time a set of potential goals and ask every student to commit themselves to a particular subset, also specifying the level of effort they are ready to expend. It may make the process more 'official' if students have a 'goal-setting logbook' in which they record the details of their set plans. An example of such a logbook is provided in Table 6.

Table 6 *Weekly goal-setting logbook*

---

1. My specific goals for this week are:

....

2. Actions or steps I will take to accomplish these goals are:

....

3. How I will know I have accomplished my goals is by:

....

4. Possible difficulties that may interfere with my accomplishing these goals and how I can overcome them are:

....

(based on Alderman 1999:95)

Strategy 21

Use goal-setting methods in your classroom.

More specifically:

- Encourage learners to select specific, short-term goals for themselves.
- Emphasise goal completion deadlines and offer ongoing feedback.

Learning contracts

One motivational method that has grown out of goal-setting theory is 'contract learning', in which a formal agreement – often termed a 'learning contract' or a 'learning itinerary' – is negotiated and ratified between teacher and student. Such contracts can vary in detail and elaborateness; besides describing a series of subgoals that lead to a larger goal and the level of effort to go with these, they may also contain specifications of the teaching method, the scheduling of various course components (e.g. tests, games, projects), and the reward or grade or other outcome. Specific contracts could, for example, detail agreement about what is to be done from the beginning to end of a project or during a term, or after completing a specific section of the curriculum or coursebook.

Although this method is time-consuming, it does ensure active teacher–student negotiation about goal-setting and it formalises students' commitment to goals (Brophy 1998). Personally, I have never used learning contracts with my students, but good friends who have done so have repeatedly told me that they are effective. Contracts are not limited to individual students; the teacher might enter into an agreement with the whole class, in which case the contract will be similar to a formalised set of 'class rules' (see Table 5 in Section 2.3), although with more emphasis on specific outcomes.

Strategy 22

Use contracting methods with your students to formalise their goal commitment.

More specifically:

- Draw up a detailed written agreement with individual students, or whole groups, that specifies what they will learn and how, and the ways by which you will help and reward them.
- Monitor student progress and make sure that the details of the contract are observed by both parties.

4.4 Protecting the learners' self-esteem and increasing their self-confidence

This section concerns a crucial aspect of motivational teaching practice, yet one that is very often ignored or played down in the classroom. The main message of the following pages can be summarised in two words: 'Build confidence!'. However, when I started to elaborate on what this 'simple' message might actually involve, the material started to grow in an almost unstoppable manner, resulting in what is the longest section in the whole book. This is partly due to the fact that the notion of 'confidence' is closely related to concepts like 'self-esteem', 'self-efficacy' and 'anxiety', which are all complex notions themselves, with whole books written about them. The rationale behind connecting all these issues to classroom motivation is that in order for students to be able to focus on learning with vigour and determination, they need to have a healthy self-respect and need to believe in themselves as learners. Self-esteem and self-confidence are like the foundations of a building: if they are not secure enough, even the best technology will be insufficient to build solid walls over them. You can employ your most creative motivational ideas, but if students have basic doubts about themselves, they will be unable to 'bloom' as learners.

If one lacks self-confidence . . .

People with a low sense of self-efficacy in a given domain perceive difficult tasks as personal threats; they dwell on their own personal deficiencies and the obstacles they encounter rather than concentrating on how to perform the task successfully. Consequently, they easily lose faith in their capabilities and are likely to give up. In contrast, a strong sense of self-efficacy enhances people's achievement behaviour by helping them to approach threatening situations with confidence, to maintain a task- rather than self-diagnostic focus during task-involvement, and to heighten and sustain effort in the face of failure.

The 'self-' issues (self-esteem, self-confidence, self-efficacy, self-worth) are particularly sensitive areas in primary/secondary school learning because students are often in the developmental age when their self-image is in an ongoing flux, and doubts and worries about oneself are more common feelings than confidence or pride. Of course, looking at these youngsters you would often be unable to tell that behind the confident and 'cool' façade there is shaky ground. Yet this is the case with most teenagers. Even cheerleaders often suffer from identity crises . . .

Well said . . .

'Teenagers are the most insecure people in the world, their lives vulnerable to a host of different pressures: pressures about dating, pressures about drugs, pressures about gangs, pressures about parents, pressures about clothing, pressures about sexuality, pressures about race, pressures about grades . . .'
(David Scheidecker and William Freeman 1999:122)

Now, imagine that amongst all the turmoil of trying to develop a new adult identity, trying to work out what they should do with their life and making the first tentative steps in exploring their own sexuality, there comes the language teacher and asks these young people to start 'babbling like a child' in an obscure language. For many teenagers, self-conscious as they are and already spending a great deal of effort saving face, that is probably the last thing they would want to do. Let's not forget that the foreign language is the only school subject in which one cannot even say a simple sentence without the danger of making a serious mistake. Can you really blame students when they decide that participating is a risk that is disproportionately big and therefore they simply opt out?

What learners will do to save face . . .

According to Covington's (1992) *self-worth theory*, it is a basic human need to maintain a sense of personal value and worth, especially in the face of competition, failure, and negative feedback (which are so typical in classrooms). This basic need generates a number of unique patterns of face-saving behaviours in school settings; in such situations students may actually stand to gain by *not* trying, that is, by deliberately withholding effort. A typical example of this is when learners spend insufficient time preparing for a test so that in the case of failure they can use the lack of sufficient striving as a mitigating excuse for poor performance, rather than having to admit a lack of competence, which would be far more damaging for the student's self-concept.

Covington and Teel (1996:27–8) list a number of other frequent failure-avoiding strategies:

- *Non-performance*: The most obvious way to avoid failure and its implications for low ability is simply not to participate.
- *Taking on too much*: Students take on so many jobs that they can never give sufficient time to any one project.
- *Setting impossibly high goals*: By setting one's aspirations very high – so high that success is virtually impossible – students can avoid the implication that they are incompetent because everyone else would also be likely to fail against such odds.
- *The academic wooden leg*: Here, individuals admit to a minor personal weakness – the proverbial wooden leg – in order to avoid acknowledging a greater feared weakness such as being incompetent. One example is to blame a failing test score on test anxiety.

The summary above has illustrated how significant but at the same time sensitive the issues of self-esteem and self-confidence are, particularly for learners who have not yet reached adulthood. The good news is that teachers *can* effect their students' self-image in a positive direction. And, in their ongoing search for purpose and identity, school children are likely to respond in a very positive manner if they realise that the language classroom is a safe place where their self-worth is protected and where they can gain confidence.

How can we provide learners with the necessary confidence-building experiences? There are several direct and less direct ways. I have found the following four main strategy types particularly useful:

- Providing experiences of success.
- Encouraging the learners.
- Reducing language anxiety.
- Teaching learner strategies.

Well said . . .

'Self-concept builds the same way muscles do, slowly and often, at first, imperceptibly.'
(Jack Canfield and Harold Clive Wells 1994:4)

Providing experiences of success

There is no better recipe for building someone's confidence than to administer regular dosages of *success*. It is a commonplace but very true that 'Success breeds success'. This suggests that a particularly important motivational strategy is creating multiple opportunities for the students to demonstrate positive features and to excel. Thus, it is worth starting the study of a new unit/issue, for example, with a task in which everybody is likely to do well, and subsequent, more demanding activities should be counterbalanced by manageable tasks. In a similar vein, the concluding activity in a unit might be one that the students have become particularly well prepared to complete.

Well said . . .

'the elusive concept of self-esteem is really spelled S * U * C * C * E * S * S. The only way true self-esteem is built is through making people successful.'
(David Scheidecker and William Freeman 1999:129)

I think it is obvious that too easy tasks beat the purpose – students will be very much aware that doing those is no big achievement. It is only when students make an effort to succeed that the pride that accompanies such achievements is powerful enough to contribute to one's sense of personal worth and self-confidence (Covington and Teel 1996). 'Just within reach' is a good rule of thumb for setting the difficulty level (Wlodkowski 1986:96).

What about language tests? After all, it is low test scores that disempower students most. This is certainly no easy question. Administering tests loses its significance if the items do not pose a real challenge to the learners. However, there is a big difference between constructing a test that tries to detect the areas that learners do not know and a test which has been designed to emphasise what learners are able to do with the L2. In addition, should someone fail, this should be treated with strict confidentiality and in a forward-pointing manner, focusing on what can be learned from the failure and how it can be avoided in the future. You may also offer various improvement options for learners who do not think they have done themselves justice (for more tips on how to reduce the demotivating effects of assessment and grades, see Section 5.4).

Strategy 23

Provide learners with regular experiences of success.

More specifically:

- Provide multiple opportunities for success in the language class.
- Adjust the difficulty level of tasks to the students' abilities and counterbalance demanding tasks with manageable ones.
- Design tests that focus on what learners can rather than cannot do, and also include improvement options.

Encouraging the learner

Self-esteem and self-confidence are social products, which means that they are created and shaped by the people around us. Starting when we are young children, our identities evolve to a great extent from the feedback we receive. Therefore, the opinion of significant figures, such as the teacher, plays an important role in reinforcing (or reducing) our self-image. This issue will be further discussed in Section 5.2 that addresses the issue of 'motivational feedback' in general. Here the focus will be only on one form of feedback: *encouragement*.

Well said . . .
'Self-esteem grows from the beliefs of others. When teachers believe in students, students believe in themselves. When those you respect think you can, *you* think you can.'
(James Raffini 1993:147)

Encouragement is the positive persuasive expression of the belief that someone has the capability of achieving a certain goal. It can explicitly make the learner aware of personal strength and abilities, or it can indirectly communicate that we trust the person. Indeed, sometimes a small personal word of encouragement can do the trick. While everybody can do with regular encouragement, you will find that some students need it more than others. A show of faith can have a powerful effect on them, and can keep them going, even against the odds, to demonstrate what they are capable of doing.

Strategy 24

Build your learners' confidence by providing regular encouragement.

More specifically:

- Draw your learners' attention to their strengths and abilities.
- Indicate to your students that you believe in their effort to learn and their capability to complete the tasks.

Reducing language anxiety

As argued before, the language classroom is an inherently face-threatening environment, with learners being expected to communicate using a severely restricted language code. As a result, language mistakes of various sorts abound in the learners' speech and the communicative content is often well below the level of their intellectual maturity. This is further augmented by the general apprehension associated with the grading system and the unease caused by the public nature of most teacher–student interaction. It is therefore quite understandable that *language anxiety* has been recurrently mentioned in the literature as a key factor that reduces motivation and achievement (cf. MacIntyre 1999).

Regrettably . . .

'Most children begin school with enthusiasm, but many begin to find it anxiety provoking and psychologically threatening. They are accountable for responding to their teachers' questions, completing assignments, and taking tests. Their performances are monitored, graded, and reported to their parents. These accountability pressures might be tolerable under conditions of privacy and consistent success, but they become threatening in classrooms where failure carries the danger of public humiliation.'
(Jere Brophy 1998:82)

How can we turn the language classroom into an 'anxiety-free zone'? The answer is relatively straightforward: by reducing or removing the factors that can lead to anxiety and fear. If your class has a generally warm and supportive climate, which has been mentioned as one of the basic motivational conditions (cf. Section 2.2), you are already halfway there. Here are some further issues to consider:

Social comparison: Few things are more detrimental to one's self-esteem than the constant threat of social comparison hanging over one's head like a sword of Damocles. This involves an excessive emphasis on comparing successful and unsuccessful learners, and can be imposed in a variety of ways in the classroom, some more subtle than others: public pronouncement of grades (sometimes only the highest and lowest), displays of selected papers and achievements, wall charts detailing student achievement and ability grouping. Even seemingly innocent feedback of the 'you are a bit behind the others' or 'you've done better than most' type can draw attention to social comparison and create a particular mindset in the student whereby everything is looked at critically through the others' (imagined) eyes.

Competition: A competitive classroom is one in which students work against each other in an attempt to outdo their classmates. This can be promoted by the scarcity of rewards (e.g. only the top 10 per cent will get a top grade) or the instructor's teaching style. In any case, this is the survival of the fittest, and for every winner there is one (or more) loser. Introducing a bit of 'healthy competition' into the classroom is often justified by claiming it brings out the best in many students. However, most motivation researchers (cf. Ames 1992; Covington 1992) would maintain that this is an unfounded myth. There is nothing 'healthy' about even a small dose of competition: 'whenever students are busy avoiding the feelings of failure, or attempting to make others fail, there is little room for true involvement in learning' (Covington and Teel 1996:108). Thus, unless in game-like activities that are not taken seriously, it is generally recommended that we play down competition amongst students and promote *cooperation* (cf. Section 4.6).

Well said . . .

'There is little reason to accept the basic premise of the argument that the world is fundamentally competitive. Quite to the contrary, the essential enabling characteristic of our society is cooperation, not competition.'
(Martin Covington and Karen Manheim Teel 1996:108)

Mistakes: A third major source of anxiety is the fear of making mistakes. In a language class this fear is so strong in some students that they are practically determined to stay silent rather than risk committing a grammatical error. I have found that language teachers can easily get into the habit of correcting every single mistake: after all, we can't help noticing these mistakes as they represent 'faulty language'; and, furthermore, most students also expect their mistakes to be corrected. Without trying to go into details about the complex issue of error correction, let me state here that modern methodologies typically recommend only the selective correction of mistakes so that student communication is not stifled, and from a motivational point of view, mistakes are not to be clamped down on but rather to be accepted as natural concomitants of learning. You can model this acceptance by dealing with your own language errors (particularly if you are a non-native teacher). The offshoot should be that 'Mistakes are okay because without mistakes there is no learning!'. And 'There is a lot of learning from mistakes!'

Mistakes . . .

'We have been conditioned through almost all our schooling that mistakes are "bad". Errors have come to signify some degree of falling short of goals, if not outright failure. Perfection is thought to be defined as errorlessness. Some foreign language teaching methods

---

> of the 1950s and 60s unfortunately held that avoidance of errors was to be admired and sought after. . . . Research has shown just the opposite to be true. . . . You can no more learn a language without making mistakes than you can learn to play tennis without ever hitting the ball into the net.'
> (H. Douglas Brown 1989:55)

Tests and assessment: Although being assessed is inevitably anxiety-provoking, the damage can be controlled by providing sufficient advance warning and information about the test, including clear specifications of the criteria that will be used for marking. During the administration of the test, students should be given plenty of time so that even the slowest students can finish comfortably. There are two more aspects of testing that are often highlighted in the literature on student-centred education. First, that in order to take the edge off potential failing, students who have not done themselves justice should be offered options to improve the final grade. Second, that the final grade should be the product of two-way negotiation (i.e. students should also be asked to express their opinion in a personal interview), preferably accompanied by the student's self-assessment (see also Section 5.4).

Strategy 25

Help diminish language anxiety by removing or reducing the anxiety-provoking elements in the learning environment.

More specifically:

- Avoid social comparison, even in its subtle forms.
- Promote cooperation instead of competition.
- Help learners to accept the fact that they will make mistakes as part of the learning process.
- Make tests and assessment completely 'transparent' and involve students in the negotiation of the final mark.

Teaching learner strategies

Confidence about one's ability to cope with the course material does not only depend on the general level of difficulty of the tasks or on the learner's perceived competence but also on the amount of support

94

Table 7 *Examples of learning strategies*

- Classifying language material into meaningful units.
- Relating new language information to concepts already in memory.
- Placing a new word/phrase in a sentence to remember it.
- Learning new vocabulary by using word cards.
- Memorising new words by means of meaningful visual imagery.
- Determining the meaning of a new expression by breaking it down into parts.
- Making a mental or written summary of the new material.
- Ordering, classifying or labelling new material.
- Relating new information to prior knowledge.
- Deciding in advance to attend to specific aspects of the language input.
- Explicitly identifying the main difficulty in a learning task.
- Regularly reviewing newly learnt language material.
- Taking notes or highlighting information.
- Regularly evaluating one's own progress in the new language.
- Seeking out or creating practice opportunities.
- Seeking help from others.
- Questioning for clarification.
- Practising new material with a friend.

(partly based on O'Malley and Chamot 1990; Oxford 1990)

available. Paramount in this respect is the role of various strategies that the teacher can present to the learners to facilitate their response to various tasks. Students can 'hang on to' these strategies when feeling insecure and the successful application of these strategies can greatly enhance their learning effectiveness.

One set of strategies learners can apply involves 'learning strategies', which refer to a range of specific learning techniques that make learning more effective. Examples include various ways of memorising vocabulary or methods to organise, practise and recycle learned material (see Table 7). I cannot offer here an overview of the extensive literature of learning strategy training (for two accessible overviews, see Oxford 1990 and Cohen 1998), but the available evidence suggests that it is possible for teachers to help students to discover for themselves the ways in which they learn best.

In a similar vein, students can also be taught *communication strategies*, which will help them to overcome difficulties in communication that are due to their limited L2 proficiency (for a review, see Cohen 1998; Dörnyei and Scott 1997; for a set of examples, see Table 8). I have found that by teaching learners practical techniques such as how to paraphrase a word that they can't remember or how to gain time to

Table 8 *Some commonly used communication strategies*

AVOIDANCE OR REDUCTION STRATEGIES

- *Message abandonment*: Leaving a message unfinished because of some language difficulty
- *Topic avoidance*: Avoiding topic areas or concepts which pose language difficulties.
- *Message replacement*: Substituting the original message with a new one because of not feeling capable of executing it.

ACHIEVEMENT OR COMPENSATORY STRATEGIES

- *Circumlocution*: Describing or exemplifying the target word you cannot remember (e.g. 'the thing you open bottles with' for 'corkscrew').
- *Approximation*: Using an alternative term which expresses the meaning of the word you cannot remember as closely as possible (e.g. 'ship' for 'sailing boat').
- *Use of all-purpose words*: Extending a general, 'empty' lexical item to contexts where specific words are lacking (e.g. the use of 'thing', 'stuff', 'make', 'do', as well as using words like 'thingie', 'what-do-you-call-it', 'what's-his-name', etc.).
- *Word-coinage*: Creating a non-existing L2 word based on a supposed rule (e.g. 'vegetarianist' for 'vegetarian').
- *Use of non-linguistic means*: Mime, gesture, facial expression or sound imitation.
- *Literal translation*: Translating literally a lexical item, an idiom, a compound word or structure from L1 to L2.
- *Foreignising*: Using an L1 word by adjusting it to L2 phonologically (i.e. with an L2 pronunciation) and/or morphologically (e.g. adding to it an L2 suffix).
- *Code switching*: Including an L1 word with L1 pronunciation or an L3 word with L3 pronunciation in L2 speech.

STALLING OR TIME-GAINING STRATEGIES

- *Use of fillers and other hesitation devices*: Using filling words or gambits to fill pauses and to gain time to think (e.g. 'well', 'now let me see', 'as a matter of fact', etc.).
- *Repetition*: Repeating a word or a string of words immediately after they were said (either by the speaker or the conversation partner).

INTERACTIONAL STRATEGIES

- *Appeal for help* – turning to the conversation partner for help either *directly* (e.g. 'What do you call. . .?') or *indirectly* (e.g. rising intonation, pause, eye contact, puzzled expression).
- *Asking for repetition*: Requesting repetition when not hearing or understanding something properly (e.g. 'Sorry?', 'Pardon?').

- *Asking for clarification*: Requesting explanation of an unfamiliar meaning structure (e.g. 'What do you mean?', 'The what?').
- *Asking for confirmation*: Requesting confirmation that one heard or understood something correctly (e.g. 'You mean?', 'Do you mean?').
- *Expressing non-understanding*: Expressing that one did not understand something properly either verbally or nonverbally (e.g. 'Sorry, I don't understand', 'I think I've lost the thread').
- *Interpretive summary*: Extended paraphrase of the interlocutor's message to check that the speaker has understood correctly (e.g. 'So what you are saying is . . .', 'Let me get this right; you are saying that . . .').

think by using filling expressions (as politicians do . . .), their confidence in participating in L2 tasks can be significantly increased.

Strategy 26

Build your learners' confidence in their learning abilities by teaching them various learner strategies.

More specifically:

- Teach students learning strategies to facilitate the intake of new material.
- Teach students communication strategies to help them overcome communication difficulties.

4.5 Allowing learners to maintain a positive social image

For most school children the main social arena in life is their school and their most important reference group is their peers. That is, school is not merely an educational environment – as many of us, teachers, would like to believe – but a context where every educational decision and event has implications about the social life of the learners:

- The impact of academic achievement is not restricted to intellectual development but it also affects a student's general self-worth and social standing in the class.
- Failure in a subject matter causes not only personal disappointment but public embarrassment.

Therefore, students' attempts to create and maintain a positive social image – which is one of the most basic human needs – will inevitably include what may seem from a purely academic point of view irrational and bizarre behaviours (such as the failure-avoiding and face-saving strategies described at the beginning of Section 4.4).

Well said . . .

'There are few influences in a student's life more powerful than the feeling of being rejected by others.'
(James Raffini 1996:9)

All these considerations suggest that a particularly effective motivational strategy is to make the learning process such that it allows learners to *maintain a positive social image* while attending to academic issues. In other words, we might be able to considerably promote motivation to learn if we manage to combine the learners' academic and social goals. This is pure common sense: no student is likely to be keen to do a task (no matter how useful it is) that puts them in a situation where they are made to look small in front of their contemporaries. In contrast, if we can provide an opportunity for everybody to play the protagonist's role in one way or another (e.g. by creating situations in which students can demonstrate their particular strength), the 'positive hero' image might work as an unprecedented stimulant.

In my own experience . . .

I became convinced about the importance of finding a protagonist's role for everybody during the course of an adult evening EFL class that I taught in the late 1980s (see Dörnyei and Gajdátsy 1989). This class mainly consisted of mature students (including, for example, a grandmother) who all studied English for some personal reason that was generally related to their careers or ambitions. There was only one young student – let's call him Ödi – who was trying to supplement his secondary school tuition by attending my course. He was barely 14 but looked younger and behaved even younger – or rather didn't behave much at all as he was silent and withdrawn most of the time. One evening we were performing short drama sketches by the British 'Monty Python' group. Ödi was given a key role in the 'parrot scene', in which a shop assistant and a customer argue in a pet shop about whether a recently bought parrot is dead or just asleep. To my delight, Ödi seemed to enjoy his

---

role: his shyness suited the humour of the sketch and the performance was a big success. However, the bigger surprise came during the next lesson: Ödi appeared to be a changed person. He carried on in the charming style he developed during the sketch the previous lesson and the level of his participation increased dramatically. By finding a suitable social style for himself, he could now concentrate on his academic goals.

You can go a long way towards protecting, and if possible enhancing, your students' social image by establishing the kind of safe and supportive classroom atmosphere that was described in Section 2.2. There are, however, some further, more specific strategies concerning what we should, and should not, do if we wish to make our classes socially desirable. The 'shoulds' involve the creation of opportunities for participation which offer students 'good' roles (i.e. ones that more or less guarantee that the participants will appear in a favourable light). These situations can be L2-related (like performing humorous sketches in the L2) but they might also involve other useful contributions to the class, such as, for example, asking a person to free a blind that got stuck (which may require one to stand on the shoulder of the other and to perform acrobatic movements). Everybody has certain strengths, and if we can find a way of associating these strengths with L2 learning or the L2 classes, we have won half the battle.

With regard to what we *should not* do, the rule of thumb is straightforward: 'Don't do anything which may result in a student losing face in front of the others!'. This means that:

- We should avoid criticisms and corrections that can be considered humiliating. Learners who are particularly in need of being motivated often have a low opinion of themselves and their efforts tend to be restricted to avoiding failures. Therefore their accomplishments should be recognised and their errors should be addressed with caution. Criticism should only be offered in private.
- We should avoid putting learners in the spotlight unexpectedly or without their agreement or before we are confident that they will be able to do themselves justice. Many students have been demotivated by the embarrassment of having to speak in the L2 in front of the class.
- We should avoid disciplining students in ways that they might perceive as humiliating (e.g. pouncing upon them when they do not listen).

> **Strategy 27**
>
> *Allow learners to maintain a positive social image while engaged in the learning tasks.*
>
> More specifically:
>
> - Select activities that contain 'good' roles for the participants.
> - Avoid face-threatening acts such as humiliating criticism or putting students in the spotlight unexpectedly.

4.6 Promoting cooperation among the learners

Encouraging cooperation between students has already been mentioned more than once (and will undoubtedly be mentioned again later) because it is related to a range of motivational practices (e.g. promoting the development of a cohesive group or supporting learner autonomy). However, it is such a powerful means of increasing student motivation that I have decided to devote a separate section to it.

Basically, cooperation is a definite 'plus'. Studies from all over the world are unanimous in claiming that students in cooperative environments have more positive attitudes towards learning and develop higher self-esteem and self-confidence than in other classroom structures. Educational theory has even proposed a teaching approach, called *cooperative learning*, which is entirely built on the concept of peer collaboration, and this approach, according to Slavin (1996:43) has been 'one of the greatest success stories in the history of educational research'. In the L2 field, various forms of peer cooperation have become well-established techniques (e.g. small group activities or project work in the spirit of communicative language teaching), which is due to the fact that peer interaction is seen in modern language teaching methodologies as a prerequisite to building the learners' communicative competence (for more about cooperative language learning, see Ehrman and Dörnyei 1998; Oxford and Nyikos 1997).

What are the reasons for the very favourable impact of cooperation on motivation? There are several:

- Cooperation fosters class group *cohesiveness* (cf. Section 2.3). When students work together they tend to like each other regardless of ethnic, cultural, class or ability differences. This is because in cooperative situations students are dependent on each other and share common goals, which in turn create a feeling of solidarity and comradely supportiveness.

- If learners are allowed to cooperate with each other towards a certain goal, their *expectancy of success* (cf. Section 3.2) is likely to be higher than if they are to work individually because they know that they can also count on their peers. The cooperating team is a powerful resource pool.
- Cooperative team work achieves a rare synthesis of *academic* and *social goals* (which was argued in the previous section to be the ideal combination from a motivational perspective): it tends to be effective in terms of learning, and it also responds directly to the students' needs for belonging and relatedness.
- In cooperative situations there is a sense of *obligation* and *moral responsibility* to the 'fellow-cooperators'. This means that peers are likely to pull each other along when motivation would be otherwise low. The joint responsibility also means that in such setups the likelihood of 'free-riding' (i.e. doing very little while reaping the benefits of others' performance) decreases.
- Cooperation is also motivating because the knowledge that one's *unique contribution* is required for the group to succeed increases one's efforts.
- Cooperative situations generally have a *positive emotional tone*, which means that they generate less anxiety and stress than other learning formats.
- Cooperative teams are by definition *autonomous* (because they have to work a lot without the immediate supervision of the teacher), and autonomy is a powerful contributor to motivation (see Section 4.7).
- The *satisfaction* that students experience (cf. Section 5.3) after they successfully complete a task together is increased by the shared experience and the joint celebration that usually follows.
- Cooperative situations increase the significance of *effort* relative to ability, because in team work the main characteristic people are judged by is their commitment to the team. This, in turn, promotes effort-based attributions, which will be a central issue when we discuss self-evaluation in Section 5.1.

What are the key features of effective cooperative tasks? The following points are most often mentioned in teachers' accounts and research papers:

1 Learners should work together in *small groups* of 3–6 members.
2 Learning is structured in a way that group members are 'positively interdependent', that is, rely on each other to be able to complete the task. This can be achieved in several ways:

- Learners work towards a *single team product* (e.g. joint performance).
- In addition to individual grades, some sort of *team score* is also calculated, and it is used to modify the individual scores (e.g. when a team has prepared together for a test which the students take individually, the individual test marks will be modified by taking into account the team's average score).
- Specific *roles* are assigned to every team member so that everybody has a specific responsibility (e.g. 'explainer', 'summariser' or 'note-taker').
- *Resources* are either limited so that they need to be shared (e.g. one answer sheet per team) or they are such that they need to be fitted together (e.g. everybody receives a different section of an article).
- Certain *class rules* are set that emphasise team responsibility (e.g. no one can proceed to some new material before everybody else in the team has completed the previous assignment).

3 Learners should be given some advance *training of group skills* (e.g. listening to each other; giving reasons in arguments; organising and coordinating the team's work) and they should be asked to reflect from time to time on how the cooperative work has gone and what could be improved.

Strategy 28

Increase student motivation by promoting cooperation among the learners.

More specifically:

- Set up tasks in which teams of learners are asked to work together towards the same goal.
- Take into account team products and not just individual products in your assessment.
- Provide students with some 'social training' to learn how best to work in a team.

4.7 Creating learner autonomy

'Autonomy' is currently a buzzword in educational psychology – it is also discussed under the label of 'self-regulation' – and during the past decade several books and articles have been published on its significance in the L2 field as well (see Benson 2001, for a recent review). Allowing a touch of cynicism, I would say that part of the popularity of the concept amongst researchers is due to the fact that educational organisations in general have been rather resistant to the kind of changes that scholars would have liked to see implemented, and research has therefore increasingly turned to analysing how to prepare learners to succeed *in spite of* the education they receive. The other side of the coin is, of course, that the theoretical arguments in favour of learner autonomy are convincing and that there is some evidence that learners who are able to learn independently may gain greater proficiency – although as Barbara Sinclair (1999:100) warns us, 'none of this evidence, in itself, is a strongly compelling argument for promoting autonomy in language learning'.

Why autonomy? A teacher's account . . .

'In the mid 1970s I started for the first time to work with [Danish] pupils of 14–16 years in unstreamed language classes. I was up against the tired-of-school attitude that this age group often displays, as well as a general lack of interest in English as a school subject. In order to survive I felt I had to change my usual teacher role. I tried to involve the pupils – or rather I forced them to be involved – in the decisions concerning, for example, the choice of classroom activities and learning materials. I soon realised that giving the learners a share of responsibility for planning and conducting teaching-learning activities caused them to be actively involved and led to better learning. It also increased their capacity to evaluate the learning process. In this way a virtuous circle was created: awareness of how to learn facilitates and influences what is being learned and gives an improved insight into how to learn.'
(Leni Dam 1995:2)

The relevance of autonomy to motivation in psychology has been best highlighted by the influential 'self-determination theory' (cf. Section 1.1), according to which the freedom to choose and to have choices, rather than being forced or coerced to behave according to someone else's desire, is a prerequisite to motivation. Autonomy is also related to group dynamics (cf. Section 2.3) in that the group's internal development and growing maturity go hand in hand with the members taking on increasing responsibility and control over their own functioning. From the point of group dynamics, involved students are increasingly autonomous students.

Interesting research . . .

Noels, Clément and Pelletier (1999) conducted a pioneering study in which they examined the motivational impact of the language teacher's communicative style. They were particularly interested in the extent to which the language teacher was perceived by the students to support their autonomy and to provide useful feedback about the learning process. The researchers found that the degree of the teachers' support of student autonomy and the amount of informative feedback they provided were in a direct positive relationship with the students' sense of self-determination (autonomy) and enjoyment, which is exactly what theoretical considerations regarding learner autonomy would suggest. Interestingly, this directive influence did not reach significance with students who pursued learning primarily for extrinsic (instrumental) reasons, which indicates that those who study a language because they have to are not as autonomy-conscious as those who do it of their own free will.

What are the main ingredients of an autonomy-supporting teaching practice? Without being comprehensive (because this is a huge topic itself with tens of thousands of printed pages devoted to it in the literature), I have found the following points crucial:

1   *Increased learner involvement in organising the learning process*: The key issue in increasing learner involvement is to share responsibility with the learners about their learning process. They need to feel that they are – at least partly – in control of what is happening to them. You can do a number of things to achieve this:
    • Allow learners *choices* about as many aspects of the learning process as possible, for example about activities, teaching materials, topics, assignments, due dates, the format and the pace of their learning, the arrangement of the furniture, or the peers they want to work with. Choice is the essence of responsibility as it permits learners to see that they are in charge of the learning experience. The difficult thing about such choices from our perspective is, however, that in order to make students feel that they are really in control, these choices need to be genuine, allowing for the fact that students may make the *wrong* decision. The only way to prevent this is to 'nurture' our students' ability to make choices by gradually expanding their opportunities for real decisions, first asking them to choose between given options from a menu, then to make modifications and changes, and finally to select goals and procedures completely on their own.

- Give students positions of *genuine authority.* Designating course responsibilities makes students fully functioning members of the class group. In traditional school settings such responsibilities are not clearly separated because the teacher takes care of all of them. However, there is no reason why many of the teacher's administrative and management functions can't be turned into student or committee responsibilities. The various leadership roles, committee memberships, and other privileges can then be rotated to give everyone a chance.

- Encourage *student contributions and peer teaching.* In my experience learners are very resourceful about finding ways to convey new material to their peers, if only to show that they can do a better job than the teacher! Some of my best seminar classes at university level have been the ones where I assigned complete sets of material to small student teams (usually a pair of students) and left it to their own devices how they went about teaching it to the others. I remember a class when the game *'Call my bluff'* was used to learn about language testing or when a huge board game was created to teach taxonomies of learning strategies.

- Encourage *project work.* When students are given complete projects to carry out, they will function in an autonomous way by definition: the teacher is not part of the immediate communication network and students are required to organise themselves, to decide on the most appropriate course of action to achieve the goal, and to devise the way in which they report their findings back to the class.

- When appropriate, allow learners to use *self-assessment* procedures (cf. Ekbatani and Pierson 2000). Self-assessment raises the learners' awareness about the mistakes and successes of their own learning, and gives them a concrete sense of participation in the learning process (for an example of a self-assessment instrument, see Table 9 in Section 5.4). I realise, of course, that in most school contexts self-assessment may not be sufficient and students are also to be assessed by you, the teacher – in such cases they may perhaps be involved in deciding *when* and *how* to be evaluated.

Well said . . .

'For a teacher to commit himself to learner autonomy requires a lot of nerve, not least because it requires him to abandon any lingering notion that he can somehow guarantee the success of his learners by his own effort.'
(David Little 1991:45)

---

2 *A change in the teacher's role*: In order to allow increased learner independence, there is a need to adopt a somewhat non-traditional teaching style, often described as the *'facilitating style'*. The teacher as a facilitator does not 'teach' in the traditional sense – that is, does not consider the students empty vessels that need to be filled with words of wisdom coming entirely from the teacher and the course-book – but views him/herself as a helper and instructional designer who leads learners to discover and create their own meanings about the world. In *The Facilitator's Handbook* (a book from which I have learnt a lot) Heron (1989) argues convincingly that – contrary to beliefs – a good facilitator is not characterised by a 'soft touch' or a 'free for all' mentality. He distinguishes three different *modes* of facilitation:

- *hierarchical*;
- *cooperative*;
- *autonomous*.

In the *hierarchical mode* facilitators exercise their power to direct the learning process *for* the group, taking full responsibility and making all the major decisions. The *cooperative mode* entails the facilitator's sharing the power and responsibilities *with* the group, prompting members to be more self-directing in the various forms of learning. In the *autonomous* mode the facilitator respects the total autonomy of the group in finding their own way and exercising their own judgement. The art of effective facilitation, according to Heron, lies in finding the right balancing and sequencing of the three modes.

Well said . . .

'Facilitation is a rigorous practice since more is at stake. It pays attention to a broader spectrum of human moves than does either Lecturing or Teaching. The move from Lecturer to Teacher to Facilitator is characterised by a progressive reduction in the psychological distance between teacher and student, and by an attempt to take more account of the learner's own agenda, even to be guided by it. Control becomes more decentralised, democratic, even autonomous, and what the Facilitator saves on controlling is spent fostering communication, curiosity, insight and relationship in the group.'
(Adrian Underhill 1999:140)

In a recent summary of learner autonomy in language education, Benson (2001) offers a clear taxonomy to summarise the variety of approaches that can be applied. He distinguishes five different types of practice to foster autonomy:

- *Resource-based approaches*, which emphasise independent interaction with learning materials (e.g. individualised learning or peer teaching).
- *Technology-based approaches*, which emphasise independent interaction with educational technologies (e.g. computers).
- *Learner-based approaches*, which emphasise the direct production of behavioural and psychological changes in the learner (e.g. various forms of strategy training – cf. Section 4.4).
- *Classroom-based approaches*, which emphasise changes in the relationship between learners and teachers in the classroom and learner control over the planning and evaluation of learning.
- *Curriculum-based approaches*, which extend the idea of control over the planning and evaluation of learning to the curriculum as a whole.

This list demonstrates well that if a teacher decides to adopt a more autonomy-supporting role, there is a wide range of approaches he/she can adopt to realise this goal.

Of course, the raising of learner autonomy is not always pure joy and fun. It involves *risks*. Some conflicts among the students or between you and the students may – and almost inevitably will – develop. In the field of group dynamics this is usually labelled the 'storming stage' of group development and it is generally believed that groups need to go through such a 'cracking of the façades' in order to achieve real maturity. It is at times like this that we teachers may panic, believe everything was a mistake, blame ourselves for our 'leniency', feel angry and resentful towards the students for not understanding the wonderful opportunity they have been offered, and thus resort to traditional authoritarian methods and procedures to 'get order'. The forewarned teacher, however, will realise that some conflicts are a natural part of the autonomous learning process, gird up their loins, and mediate and negotiate the group through the storm (Dörnyei and Malderez 1997).

Problems you may encounter . . .

- It might be difficult to bring learners to make decisions and accept responsibility for these decisions.
- It might be difficult to respect the students' right to make 'wrong' decisions.

- It may not be easy to introduce group work among pupils who have never worked in groups before.
- You may not find enough ready-made activities in the course-book that are suitable for autonomous learning and have to spend some time designing new ones.
- It may be difficult for you to realise that you can't be everywhere at the same time.
- It may be (and in fact it is) scary to relinquish the traditional means of classroom control and rely on new or modified methods of discipline.
- In general, it might be difficult for you to 'let go' and trust the pupils' abilities to 'take hold'.

(partly based on Dam 1995)

Although I am a believer in learner autonomy, I think it is useful to conclude this section with Good and Brophy's (1994:228) word of caution:

> For one thing, the simplest way to ensure that people value what they are doing is to maximise their free choice and autonomy – let them decide what to do and when and how to do it. However, schools are not recreational settings designed primarily to provide entertainment; they are educational settings that students are required to come to for instruction in a prescribed curriculum. Some opportunities exist for teachers to take advantage of existing motivation by allowing students to select activities according to their own interests, but most of the time teachers must require students to engage in activities that they would not have selected on their own.

Strategy 29

Increase student motivation by actively promoting learner autonomy.

More specifically:

- Allow learners real choices about as many aspects of the learning process as possible.
- Hand over as much as you can of the various leadership/teaching roles and functions to the learners.
- Adopt the role of a facilitator.

4.8 Promoting self-motivating learner strategies

The offshoot of the last section on learner autonomy was (hopefully) that it is beneficial – both from the point of view of motivation and learning effectiveness – to encourage learners to take increasing control over their own learning process. What if we apply the same self-regulating principle to the control over one's motivation? Is there a way of getting learners to take personal control of the motivational conditions and experiences that shape their own commitment to learning? In other words, can we envisage ways of getting the learners to *motivate themselves*? A positive answer would be of considerable practical importance because most of the discussion in the motivation literature tends to focus on the *teacher's* responsibility and role in stimulating student motivation and, therefore, by enlisting the students' help, the range and effectiveness of motivational strategies could be greatly increased.

What do you think?

'Now, however, in the age of learner-centredness in education and of learner autonomy in particular, it may be that the teacher's own agenda needs to change. After all, the appropriate question no longer seems to be *how can we motivate our learners?* but *how can we help learners to motivate themselves?*'
(Ema Ushioda 1996:2)

It is not utterly naïve to think that students can do some of our motivational job. Just consider the fact that in certain classrooms even under adverse conditions and without any teacher assistance, some learners are more successful in keeping up their goal commitment than others. How do they do it? The answer is that they apply certain self-management skills to overcome environmental distractions or competing/distracting emotional or physical needs/states; in short, they motivate themselves. And if they can do it, surely others can do it as well, particularly if we provide some coaching. This assumption about students' self-motivating capacity has received confirmation during the past decade. Inspired by the pioneering work of two German psychologists, Julius Kuhl and Heinz Heckhausen (e.g. Heckhausen 1991, Heckhausen and Kuhl 1985, Kuhl 1987), recent research in educational psychology has increasingly turned to exploring what the learners can do to 'save' the action when the initial motivation is flagging (see Snow, Corno and Jackson 1996).

Quite so!

'The world is replete with enchanting distractions for even the most eager of students. Schools are complex social networks as well as places of work. Homes provide children with television, computer games, and compact discs. After-school clubs engulf what little spare time children have. To succeed academically, students must learn to cope with the competition between their social and intellectual goals and to manage and control the range of other distractions that arise.'
(Lyn Corno 1994:248)

Based on Kuhl's (1987) and Corno and Kanfer's (1993) taxonomies I would suggest that self-motivating strategies are made up of five main classes:

1   *Commitment control strategies*
2   *Metacognitive control strategies*
3   *Satiation control strategies*
4   *Emotion control strategies*
5   *Environmental control strategies*

In the following I will explain and exemplify each class separately. I will supplement my own experiences by drawing on the work of Baumeister (1996) Corno (1993), Corno and Kanfer (1993), Garcia and Pintrich (1994) and Kuhl (1987). You may also notice that some of the strategies listed will be similar to 'affective learning strategies' conceptualised by Oxford (1990) and O'Malley and Chamot (1990).

Commitment control strategies

Commitment control strategies refer to conscious techniques that help to preserve or enhance the learners' original goal commitment. This can happen by means of:

* *Keeping in mind favourable expectancies or positive incentives and rewards*: By consciously imagining the successful outcome we can re-energise our striving for the goal (e.g. a film director fantasising about receiving an Oscar for the film he/she is working on).

> **'I could go to the Olympics . . .' What motivated Olympic athlete Marilyn King?**
>
> 'Then something happened that changed her life. The Olympic committee was there to select athletes to work with. They chose two girls Marilyn had beaten. One was a fine athlete who had just performed badly on the day of the competition. However, Marilyn knew she was better than the other athlete. Of course, Marilyn was disappointed but reasoned that "If they chose her, and I beat her, that means that I could go to the Olympics. *I could go to the Olympics!*". This last phrase ran through her head over and over again when she returned home. She said it as she ran around the track and imagined actually walking one day into the Olympic stadium on opening day. Suddenly training become easier and she found herself more motivated. . . . Marilyn says now that most people think that Olympic athletes have a lot of *will-power* and *determination* and that's what enables them to work so hard. She says no, it's not that; it's the vision. It's the power of an image that inspires great passion and excitement – so much that you have enormous energy to do what you want. . . . She started bringing together other ex-Olympians to find out if they had had similar experiences. She discovered that most Olympians had a very clear vision of what they wanted and that this vision was constantly present. The vision (or goal or outcome) also inspired great passion and excitement. The vision and the passion inspired them to take a lot of action, over and over again. To do something about it . . .'
> (Tim Murphey 1998b: 61–2)

- *Focusing on what would happen if the original intention failed*: Sometimes imagining the perceived negative consequences of abandoning the action may activate enough energy to keep us going.

Metacognitive control strategies

Metacognitive control strategies refer to conscious techniques used by the learner to monitor and control concentration and to stop procrastination. Some examples are as follows:

- *Giving oneself regular self-reminders to concentrate*, such as 'Concentrate, you're losing your edge/grip!' or 'Come on, just a little bit more!'.
- *Imagining the potential consequences of a lack of concentration*: Thinking about the consequences of possible mistakes that can be the

result of carelessness might provide the necessary push at times when our attention is lagging. An intensified version of this strategy is to tell ourselves to do the work as if our life depended on it.

- *Giving oneself regular self-reminders of the deadline*: Regularly checking our progress against the time frame and threatening ourselves with missing the deadline works for many people (but not everybody).
- *Intentionally ignoring attractive alternatives or irrelevant aspects*: Adopting a narrow-minded outlook by only focusing on things that are in direct relationship with what one is preoccupied with and simply screening out irrelevant stimuli is a strategy that some people can very effectively apply. The irrelevant stimuli can include anything from a crying baby to emerging new opportunities (or, in my case, two young boys jumping on top of me while I was trying to prepare the final version of this part of the manuscript . . .).
- *Identifying recurring distractions and developing defensive routines*: It may be a useful exercise with long-term effects to first observe ourselves for a while and identify the kind of intrusive thoughts and distractions that cause our attention to drift away, and then to develop a self-talk response that will keep our mind on target.
- *Cutting short any purposeless or counterproductive procrastination*: Sometimes prolonged rumination may be an obstacle to action or may even undermine the pursuit of the goal. This is when adopting a *'let's not think about it any more but get down to doing it'* attitude might be necessary.
- *Using starter rituals to get into focus*: Setting up your equipment, checking a web site on the computer before getting down to work, clearing one's desk, etc. can often get us into the appropriate mind frame.
- *Focusing on the first steps to take*: By ignoring the complexity of the overall issue and narrowing down our attention to the very first things to do, we might concentrate sufficient energy to get started.

Satiation control strategies

Once an activity has lost its novelty, *satiation* might become a real danger. This is especially true of routine tasks, which can soon appear increasingly boring. *Satiation strategies* are intended to add extra attraction, or spice, to the task. Here are some recipes:

- *Add a twist to the task*: Think of some changes in doing the task that will make it more fun or more challenging and demanding. This can involve reordering certain action sequences; varying the context;

introducing or changing the rhythm/pace; setting artificial records and trying to break them; trying to surpass self-imposed quotas; turning recurring difficulties into challenges that need to be taken up; or even performing the action with an artistic sense (i.e. adding aesthetic qualities to the functional ones).

Mary Poppins knew . . .

'It's a game, isn't it, Mary Poppins?'
'Well, it depends on your point of view. You see, in every job that must be done there is an element of fun. You find the fun and – snap! – the job's a game. And every task you undertake becomes a piece of cake . . .'
(From the 1964 Disney motion picture)

- *Use your fantasy to liven up the task*: This strategy can take many forms. You can treat the task as a game, creating imaginary scenarios; you can treat objects as various personalities; or you can offer yourself mental self-rewards or self-imposed penance.

How did she do it?

'Mary was a friend I had in college. Without studying much, she always made really good grades. It was a mystery to me. I wondered how she did it, so I began observing her more closely . . .
Some of her classes were not really interesting to her, but still she wanted to learn and to make good grades. So she pretended (and then actually believed) that what her professors were saying was *extremely* interesting. Then she became excited about telling everybody about it . . .'
(Tim Murphey 1998b:21)

Emotion control strategies

Certain emotional states or moods – such as anxiety, fear or hopelessness – may disrupt or inhibit action and may undermine our determination, whereas others will put things in an optimistic, positive light. By means of *emotion control strategies* we can manage the obtrusive states and can also consciously generate emotions that will be conducive to implementing the intentions. Several strategies have been identified that will help us achieve these goals:

- *Generating useful diversions*: When pressure gets to us, we should try and recall something pleasant and positive to defuse the threat and to set our mind on a new track. Focusing on an unrelated but absorbing issue can also work. Alternatively, we can do something more physical to the same effect, such as singing a song or going for a quick walk.
- *Self-affirmation* involves counteracting someone's negative evaluation of something we have done by consciously activating positive images of ourselves in other domains (e.g. recalling talents and strength). Reminding ourselves of our resources and remembering times when we have done this kind of thing before also helps when feeling incapable, small or vulnerable.
- *Constructing positive narratives of events* involves 'explaining away' a negative episode by placing it into a larger narrative in which we are described in a more positive light. A typical example of this is when someone mitigates a failure by emphasising the positive aspect of avoiding an even greater failure.
- *Self-encouragement* involves positive self-talk, patting oneself on the back for good work and urging some further achievement.
- *Finding humorous elements* in a less-than-amusing situation is a conscious strategy that can very effectively lighten up any kind of misery.
- *Using relaxation and meditation techniques*. People can learn how to control their physical reactions and relax their body and their mind, for example, by consciously slowing down their breathing in stressful situations, making it steadier and deeper.
- *Counting to ten* before blowing up with anger is a traditional and rather effective way of controlling our temperament.
- *Sharing your feelings with someone else* in order to elicit help to process them.
- *Praying*.

Environmental control strategies

Environmental control strategies are partly concerned with eliminating negative environmental influences and partly with exploiting positive environmental influences by making the environment your ally in your pursuit of a difficult goal. The first aspect is straightforward: the fewer distracting factors there are around you, the more likely you are to reach your goal. Distractions that need to be eliminated can be of two kinds:

- environmental sources of interference (such as noise, friends);
- environmental temptations (such as a packet of cigarettes when you want to give up smoking).

Positive environmental influences are less straightforward. They do not exist but must be created. The point is to use environmental or social pressure to support you in the pursuit of your goal or to make it difficult for you to abandon the intention, for example by:

- Inviting a working party or arranging a meeting with the explicit purpose of getting the work started.
- Making a promise or a public commitment to do or not to do something.
- Getting yourself to reach a 'point of no return' situation.
- Asking friends to help you (e.g. not to allow you to do something).

Self-motivating strategy training

Although students do develop or discover some self-motivating strategies for themselves, these are often limited in number and variety. Therefore, an important part of any motivational teaching practice is to raise the learners' awareness of relevant strategies and to remind them at appropriate times of the usefulness of these. Self-motivating strategy training should broadly follow the procedures that have been developed for the training of learning strategies. The following is a template to outline the six main phases of such a programme:

1 Find out which self-motivating strategies your students already use and discuss these with them.
2 Suggest and model some new strategies for each of the five areas discussed above.
3 Provide a rationale for strategy use; learners will only take the trouble applying strategies and developing new ones if they become convinced about their usefulness.
4 Provide guided exercises or experiences to help students to put the strategies into practice.
5 Encourage students to develop their own strategies.
6 Organise *'sharing sessions'*: From time to time ask students to share the strategies they have generated or found particularly useful. Because of their direct involvement in the learning process, students often have fresh insights they can share with their peers in simplified terms. In addition, personalised self-motivating strategies are often quite amusing and students rather enjoy sharing them.

> *Sample activities from a volitional (i.e. self-motivating) strategy training programme at Teachers College, New York*
>
> 1 Teacher and students list prominent disturbances to working and studying at home and in class. Then they discuss ways for the students to handle these distractions and protect their concentration.
> 2 Teacher models/demonstrates both effective and ineffective responses to a distracting situation.
> 3 Students will demonstrate their knowledge of various effective and ineffective strategies by analysing prepared scenarios as part of a 20-item quiz that requires the identification and classification of more effective strategies.
> 4 Using written scenarios, small groups of students role play effective strategic responses to distracting or difficult work conditions. Peer audiences identify and evaluate the actors' choice of strategies.
> 5 Teacher reminds students that he/she will be looking for evidence of strategy use. Several tasks are targeted for teacher observation over a three-week period and the extent of improvement in task efficiency and resource management is determined. Students also perform self-evaluation, after which the teacher and the students compare notes.
>
> (source: Lyn Corno 1994:245–6)

Strategy 30

Increase the students' self-motivating capacity.

More specifically:

- Raise your students' awareness of the importance of self-motivation.
- Share with each other strategies that you have found useful in the past.
- Encourage students to adopt, develop and apply self-motivating strategies.

5 Rounding off the learning experience: Encouraging positive self-evaluation

In the previous chapters we have analysed ways of creating the basic motivational conditions, generating initial motivation and maintaining and protecting existing motivation. There is only one main motivational issue we have not talked about yet: the learners' appraisal of and reactions to their own past performance. It is a characteristic of humans that rather than looking forward and only concentrating on forth-coming challenges, they spend a great deal of time looking back, evaluating what they have done and how well it went, while trying to draw lessons for the future. In this way the past becomes closely tied to the future and, accordingly, a very important aspect of motivating learners is to help them to deal with their past in a way that it will promote rather than hinder future efforts.

All right, you may say, I can accept that what we have done in the past is related to what we will do in the future, but what's the point of talking about this? There isn't an awful lot we can do about what has already happened. The problem with this argument is that it does not take the *subjective nature* of human evaluation into account. Students' appraisal of their past performance does not only depend on the absolute level of success they have achieved but also on *how* they interpret their achievement. Have you ever seen people who were bursting with confidence and satisfaction even though what they actually produced should not have given any reason for it? Or people who seem to be constantly dissatisfied in spite of the high quality of their work? In such cases there is a very obvious mismatch between the standard of one's actual performance and how it is evaluated by the person him/herself, but looking at our past through a subjective lens is not restricted to extreme cases only; to a certain extent we all receive a slightly distorted picture.

In this chapter we are going to look at how teachers can help learners to consider their own achievement in a more positive light. More specifically, we will examine:

- how to teach learners to explain their past successes and failures in a constructive way;
- how to help them to take more satisfaction in their successes and progress;
- the characteristics of the kind of feedback that best promotes their ongoing learning;
- the controversial effects of the rewards and grades dispensed in class.

5.1 Promoting motivational attributions

The term 'attribution' has been used in psychology to refer to the explanation people offer about why they were successful or, more importantly, why they failed in the past. Because researchers have found that these subjective explanations play an important role when people start planning their future actions, a whole psychological theory has been constructed around attributions, called – not surprisingly – *'attribution theory'* (cf. Section 1.1). This is an area that non-psychologists are usually not familiar with, even though it is claimed by many that attributions lie at the very heart of motivation to learn, and attribution research was certainly the dominant approach in educational psychology in the 1980s.

It's true . . .

'The attributional explanation for motivation is one that teachers, parents, coaches, and counsellors find especially useful. As one student who had learned about attribution in another class cautioned his classmates, "You will never look at yourselves the same way again after learning about attribution".'
(Kay Alderman 1999:ix)

Let me offer an illustration of the power of attributions. We have all seen learners who won't even try to succeed any more because they simply do not believe that they can. Extreme cases characterised by this lack of confidence in one's potentials have been termed 'learned helplessness' in the psychological literature and there is an agreement among researchers that once students reach this stage, it is very difficult to get them out of it. What's wrong with these learners? How did they 'learn to be helpless'? One basic problem with them is that they interpret their past learning experiences in a debilitating manner. They may attribute their past failures to stable and uncontrollable causes, such as the *lack of ability*, rather than factors that are changeable and within their control, such as the *too little work* or *insufficient knowledge/use of appropriate strategies*. From this perspective it is understandable that they do not try very hard, since there isn't much point fighting the invincible. Attribution theory offers us a framework that can help us to interpret student claims like 'I can't do maths – I'm too stupid for it . . .', and by understanding what is behind such claims, we may start changing the negative attitudes.

What do students typically attribute their successes and failures to? As Graham (1994) summarises, the most common attributions in school environments are:

- ability
- effort
- task difficulty
- luck
- mood
- family background
- help or hindrance from others.

Among these, particularly two – *ability* and *effort* – have been identified as the most influential perceived causes in western culture. Attributing past failures to the former is extremely harmful ('I simply don't have a talent for languages'), whereas believing that we haven't done ourselves justice in the past because we did not work hard enough is a *constructive attribution* since the logical conclusion a student will draw is 'I will work harder!'

Of course, when it comes to explaining successes, we have an altogether different story: it is much better to believe that you have done well because you are smart (i.e. have the high abilities) than because you were ready to toil away relentlessly (i.e. put in the effort).

Well said . . .

'In short, the ideal motivational scenario is one in which students attribute positive outcomes to personal ability, and negative outcomes to temporary shortcomings that can be remedied.'
(Ema Ushioda 1996:13)

Attribution theory is particularly relevant to the study of language learning for two reasons:

1 *Failure* in learning an L2 is very common: In spite of the great

number of people spending a considerable amount of time studying foreign languages worldwide, only relatively few will ever reach a level of L2 proficiency that satisfies them without any reservations – the regrettable fact is that most people fail in at least one L2 during their lifetime (personally speaking, my varying degree of success in English and German has been well counterbalanced by failures in Russian, Latin, Spanish and Portuguese). Furthermore, even successful learners frequently get into frustrating situations when they cannot use the L2 as well as they would hope to. With failure being such a common experience, the way people process these failures is bound to have a very strong general impact.

2   The ability to learn an L2 – often called *language aptitude* – is a notion that people in general are familiar with and therefore refer to regularly. This means that it is all too easy to come up with negative ability-attributions, such as 'I don't have a knack for languages' or 'I am not a natural linguist', even if this is not the case at all.

Attribution training is intended to prevent students from making deliberating attributions and to change negative attributional styles. The underlying assumption is that, as Covington (1998:75) summarised, 'it is not so much the event of failure that disrupts academic achievement as it is the meaning of failure. Thus, rather than minimising failure, educators should arrange schooling so that falling short of one's goals will be interpreted in ways that promote the will to learn.' Indeed, depending on how one perceives it, failure can increase one's work morale or it may decrease it. Our job, then, is to try and ensure that the former happens.

Promoting effort attributions

The essence of promoting motivational attributions can be summarised in a short sentence: *encourage students' effort attributions.* This suggestion means, to start with, that we ought to play down the importance of ability (except, perhaps, after successes, but even then effort should also be emphasised). Referring to ability too much is a dangerous practice because if we start placing emphasis on ability in the classroom, some learners will inevitably come out badly in this respect. Highlighting the role of effort, on the other hand, is safe: it facilitates future achievement and everybody has an equal chance to it. If we can make students believe that higher levels of effort in general offer a possibility for success, they will persist in spite of the inevitable failures that accompany learning.

> **Well said . . .**
> 'students should never be allowed to fail at tasks until they have a
> reasonable chance to succeed. If they do, they have no choice but to
> attribute their failure to lack of ability and will therefore stop
> trying.'
> (James Raffini 1993:107)

How can we encourage effort attributions? Here are some suggestions:

- *Provide effort feedback*: The most effective means towards promoting
  effort attributions is the *feedback* we give to our students. In failure
  situations, the general advice is that we should emphasise the *low
  effort* exerted as being a strong reason for underachievement because
  this communicates to students that they can do better in the future.
  What about those situations when a student fails even though he/she
  has put reasonable effort into his/her work? In such cases it is also
  important to emphasise that effort needs to be complemented with
  sufficient *skills* and *strategies*, which can be mastered (Pintrich and
  Schunk 1996).
- *Refuse to accept ability attributions*: When students verbalise attributions to low ability (e.g. 'I'm not good at languages'), gently but
  firmly refuse to accept this explanation. Instead, offer the alternative
  explanation that the student has failed to succeed because he/she has
  addressed the task using ineffective strategies and because he/she did
  not persist long enough. Point out that in average school learning
  there are no subject areas that cannot be mastered to a reasonable
  extent through the combination of effort and strategies even by low-
  ability students, and make it clear that you have confidence in the
  student's abilities.
- *Model effort-outcome linkages*: Describe personal experiences in
  which you managed to accomplish a difficult task by trying hard to
  succeed. Elicit similar stories from the learners themselves. They
  might even read true stories and biographies describing individuals
  who have attained goals through effort and discuss with them after-
  wards why these people have succeeded. Another way of modelling
  effort attributions is to demonstrate tasks by thinking out loud as you
  work through them. When you encounter setbacks in performing
  everyday classroom activities, model confidence that you will succeed
  if you persist and if you find a better strategy.
- *Encourage learners to offer effort explanations*: Ushioda (1996)
  points out – quite rightly – that the motivational belief in the value of
  individual effort will have a much surer foundation if it is expressed

by the learners *themselves* in their *own* words. We can encourage this by providing appropriate prompting and support. For example, we may ask the learners to explain what they found particularly challenging about a language task, what strategies they used to meet this challenge and what they learned from the experience.

- *Make effort and perseverance a class norm*: Wlodkowski (1986) suggests that by making consistent comments to that effect, effort and perseverance can come to be seen as valued components of the class ethos. Any remark that says 'I like the way you try' or 'That was a nice piece of effort' can emphasise the general importance of effortful behaviour and contribute to making it a classroom norm. To promote this norming process, from time to time, when there is a good opportunity, you may spend some whole-class time discussing the role that effort and persistence play in overcoming failures and in producing productive work. The optimal offshoot of these discussions is the recognition that persistence eventually pays off and every learner can succeed if they apply themselves. If some students remain doubtful, reassure them that you will provide extra help if you can see that they are trying.

Strategy 31

Promote effort attributions in your students.

More specifically:

- Encourage learners to explain their failures by the lack of effort and appropriate strategies applied rather than by their insufficient ability.
- Refuse to accept ability attributions and emphasise that the curriculum is within the learners' ability range.

5.2 Providing motivational feedback

Besides grades (cf. Section 5.4), it is the *feedback* you give your students in class or on their written papers that has the most salient role in bringing about changes in their learning behaviours. However, from a motivational perspective not every type of feedback is equally effective and on occasions, if we are not careful enough, our comments might be counterproductive. The significance of teacher feedback has already been addressed in more than one place before, for example in Section 4.4 when we discussed the importance of *encouragement* in boosting the learner's self-confidence, and in the previous section where different ways of promoting effort attributions were described. However, there is more to feedback.

First of all, feedback is not just a decoration on the cake or an additional asset that's worth having. It is an essential ingredient of learning. Ford (1992) calls this the *'Feedback Principle'*, stating that people simply cannot continue to make progress toward their personal goals in the absence of relevant feedback information. When there is no feedback, it is easy for goals – even important goals – to lose salience and priority, and eventually end up 'on the shelf'.

Well said . . .

'Without feedback, motivational headquarters is effectively shut off from action – it can only guess, using *feedforward* information, how the instrumental troops are doing in their efforts to carry out system directives.'
(Martin Ford 1992:210)

What is effective feedback like from a motivational point of view? Three things need to be highlighted here:

- First, feedback can have – when it is due and appropriate – a *gratifying function*, that is, by offering praise it can increase learner satisfaction and lift the learning spirit. This aspect will be addressed in the second part of this chapter (Sections 5.3–4).
- Second, by communicating trust and encouragement, feedback can promote a positive self-concept and self-confidence in the student (this aspect was covered in Section 4.4)
- Third – and this is going to be the focus of the current section – motivational feedback should prompt the learner to reflect constructively on areas that need improvement and identify things that he/she can do to increase the effectiveness of learning. This kind of feedback is often termed *'positive information feedback'* (Raffini, 1993).

Yes!

A good rule of thumb: *pass along to your students any compliments you have heard about them!*

'Positive information feedback' involves positive, descriptive feedback regarding student strengths, achievements, progress and attitudes. Most importantly, this feedback provides students with information rather than judgements against external standards or peer achievement (which is the main feature of *'controlling feedback'* – see Good and Brophy 1994) . To provide an illustration, controlling feedback would involve, for example, comparing a student's rather low test score to the average score of the class, highlighting the need to work harder to be able to catch up with the others, whereas information feedback would compare the same score to the student's previous achievement, noting positive or negative trends, and at the same time identifying areas that were okay and areas that the student should focus on to improve on their progress. One particularly useful aspect of information feedback is when it also provides information on how successfully the learners were applying various *strategies* and how their strategy use was improving their performance.

Three types of teacher feedback that can backfire and have negative consequences

- Communicating pity after failure.
- The offering of praise after success in *easy* tasks.
- Unsolicited offers of help, particularly 'gratuitous help' such as supplying answers outright.

(based on Graham 1994)

Finally, two more suggestions concerning the effectiveness of feedback:

- Alison (1993) warns us that in the 'general bustle of the lesson' or in our concern to 'get through the work' we can easily restrict our attention to spotting mistakes and misdemeanours and overlook positive contributions, whereas from a motivational perspective the exact opposite would be more favourable. In order to stop students from developing a 'Why bother?' attitude when their positive contributions have gone unnoticed, we need to keep on the alert for even the slightest manifestation of forward-pointing contributions. This may be especially important with learners whose motivational basis is rather shaky. With problem students we must see through their misbehaviour to find attributes that we can acknowledge and support.
- Feedback that is made promptly available is far more effective than delayed feedback because in the former case the learner has an 'online' awareness of his/her progress. This is, in fact, one reason why computer-assisted instruction can be so motivating.

> **Strategy 32**
>
> *Provide students with positive information feedback.*
>
> More specifically:
>
> - Notice and react to any positive contributions from your students.
> - Provide regular feedback about the progress your students are making and about the areas which they should particularly concentrate on.

5.3 Increasing learner satisfaction

I have noticed in myself and also in many others that we tend to show far less emotion when something goes right than when it goes wrong. And, at least in myself, this is not the sign of humble modesty but rather a lack of sufficient attention to success. When I am in an 'action mode' I tend to look only forward, constantly monitoring the oncoming challenges and working out strategies to meet them, and when something has been successfully completed it rarely elicits more than a mental tick because my attention is already on the next obstacle to overcome. I suppose that many people operate like that. The problem with such a challenge-oriented attentional mode is that we miss out on the celebratory part and reduce the amount of satisfaction we may feel. We take accomplishments for granted and only make the errors in the learning machinery tangible. This can result in the students having a distorted picture where difficulties are overemphasised, which can prevent them from feeling good about their achievement and thereby from building a positive self-image and motivational belief structure. Celebrations and satisfaction are crucial motivational building blocks because they validate effort, affirm the entire learning process, reinforce the value of the experience, and in general provide the bright spots along the road towards the ultimate goal.

> *Well said . . .*
>
> 'Recognition of success is not juvenile – in fact, it is what we all expect from life, and the wise teacher, in a non-threatening manner, takes full advantage of this most common human desire.'
> (David Scheidecker and William Freeman 1999:105)

I am sure that few people would argue with the above and yet we continuously 'under-celebrate'. An effective motivational strategy is therefore to 'over-celebrate'. How do we do it? How can we make success memorable? The first thing most people would think of is probably offering rewards – a controversial issue that will be discussed in the next section. If not rewards then what? Luckily, as in most motivational areas, we have a variety of techniques and approaches to be chosen from:

- *Monitor and recognise your learners' accomplishments*: Make sure that the students' personal 'milestones' do not go unnoticed. Most students welcome public recognition, but you may also want to send them short private notes – writing comments on their written papers provides a good and unobtrusive opportunity for this and these personal comments are usually highly appreciated by the addressees.
- *Take time to celebrate success*: It is usually time well spent to celebrate successes and achievement in class. A good rule of thumb is that 'regardless of how small, every success must be celebrated' (Scheidecker and Freeman 1999:106). Celebrations often involve giving *praise*, which is welcome if it focuses on our appreciation of the students' efforts and accomplishments rather than on their role in pleasing the teacher. Applause and standing ovations are great if they do not embarrass the recipient.
- *Regularly take stock of progress*: Learning a foreign language is a lengthy, continuous process in which progress is rarely conspicuous. For example, adding another 500 new words to one's vocabulary will not automatically lead to a dramatic improvement in one's performance. It is worthwhile therefore to stop from time to time and look back on what has already been achieved.
- *Include tasks which involve the public display or performance of the outcome*: Certain tasks such as role-play activities or the making of a visual product allow students automatically to share and to publicly display their projects and skills. And few things are more satisfying than public attention and (hopefully) recognition.
- *Make progress tangible*: Once progress/accomplishments have been recognised and acknowledged we may want to increase their motivational impact by making them *tangible*. And nothing is more tangible than some sort of visual summary, such as an accomplishment album, a wall chart, a public display of a checklist of skills and knowledge areas with coloured symbols to mark what has been done. The visual summary can also take the form of a student anthology, and the class newsletter is another good forum for a range of student products.

- *Provide a reinforcing event for positive closure at the end of significant units of learning*: This strategy, highlighted by Wlodkowski (1986), is another good way of breaking up the lengthy learning process into meaningful segments, with a final event marking and celebrating the successful accomplishment of each larger section. The 'reinforcing event' can range from a small gesture, such as thanking learners for their cooperation, to something much more spectacular, such as an awards ceremony or a term-closing party.

Strategy 33

Increase learner satisfaction.

More specifically:

- Monitor student accomplishments and progress, and take time to celebrate any victory.
- Make student progress tangible by encouraging the production of visual records and arranging regular events.
- Regularly include tasks that involve the public display of the students' skills.

5.4 Offering rewards and grades in a motivating manner

To conclude our survey of motivational techniques, we have arrived at what is probably the most well-known but also the most controversial area, the role of *rewards* and *grades*. Let me start the discussion by admitting that motivational psychologists in general do not like rewards (or grades, which are one type of rewards). This is all the more remarkable because teachers do, and dispense them liberally for good behaviour and academic performance. Most teachers feel that it is a positive thing to reward their students' praiseworthy efforts and accomplishments. What is more, rewards are amazingly versatile and usable: they can be applied in just about any teaching context for tasks as diverse as memorising poetry to completing research reports. Accordingly, many kinds of rewards are used in schools, ranging from highly tangible ones such as sweets, through various presents and certificates, to grades of various forms. These rewards, particularly grades, then enjoy great credibility among parents and college admission or personnel officers.

Well said . . .

'Rewards and punishment are too often the only tools available in the motivational arsenal of many teachers. Although these two timeworn tactics can control many student behaviours, their indiscriminate use can seriously undermine students' intrinsic motivation for the activities and behaviours being controlled.'
(James Raffini 1996:1)

To counterbalance these assumed merits, most psychologists would respond that rewards more often than not actually do motivation a great deal of *damage*. They would claim that real motivational practices do not have to rely on dispensing rewards, which they see as the most simplistic motivational tool: rewards do not increase the inherent value of the task or the task outcome, and neither do they concern other important learning aspects such as the learning process, the learning environment or the learner's self-concept. Instead, all rewards do is simply attach a piece of 'carrot or stick' to the task. By doing so, they divert the students' attention away from the real task and the real point of learning. 'We don't want students to read Shakespeare just because they can earn themselves brownie points for each play they have "done"', says the idealist motivation scholar; and then carries on, 'And neither do we want students to do tasks only to avoid punishment.' But, of course, the pragmatic teacher has a ready reply to these concerns: 'Surely it's better for someone to read Shakespeare's plays for brownie points than not to read them at all. And participating in the classroom to avoid punishment must be infinitely better than playing truant instead.'

Well said . . .

'The improper use of incentives can create a failure-prone environment in which the playing field is tilted against most students. When fear is the stimulus, there are few winners in the learning game. And even the winners may pay a heavy price.'
(Martin Covington and Karen Manheim Teel 1996:6)

In the following I will look into the 'reward controversy' in more detail. I will examine the way rewards and grades work, what effects they have on student motivation and, most importantly, how they can be used in a more motivating manner.

Rewards

What can we say about rewards? Are they the necessary evil or are they beneficial when properly used? As mentioned earlier in this book, in an ideal world students would need no external incentives such as rewards because they would be driven by their inborn curiosity and the joy they gain from the learning process itself. However, we are not living (or at least teaching) in an ideal world and, in fact, many classrooms are becoming less and less ideal. This being the case, I think that rewards can constitute powerful motivational tools which would be a real luxury to ignore.

First of all, what kind of rewards are we talking about? Even if we disregard praise and celebration that have been discussed in the previous section and grades that will be analysed separately below, the variety is still impressive:

- material rewards, such as sweets, ice cream and other consumables, money, various school prizes (e.g. books, pencils, bookmarks, trinkets);
- special privileges, opportunities and perks, such as choosing activities or stories, extra play time, use of special equipment (e.g. computer) or facilities (e.g. library, gym);
- awards and other recognitions, such as honour rolls, notice board displays, gold stars;
- teacher rewards, such as special attention, personalised relationship, special times spent together.

What are the potential dangers of rewards? There are three main points mentioned recurrently in the psychology literature:

1 It has been well documented that if you start offering rewards for something that students were already doing for their own reasons, the reward may undermine the existing motivation (Deci and Ryan 1985).
2 As Brophy (1998) summarises, when people start concentrating on the reward rather than on the task, they often overlook the actual values associated with the task itself.
3 Whenever students are offered salient rewards for doing tasks they can easily succumb to the 'mini-max principle' (Covington and Teel 1996), whereby they attempt to maximise rewards with a minimum of effort.

Are these problems insurmountable? Not necessarily. In certain circumstances rewards seem to work fine. For example, it is a relatively common scenario that someone who has originally taken up a task purely for the sake of a reward develops a personal liking to the activity and carries it on of his/her free will. This suggests that whether or not a reward supports or hinders motivation does not lie in the reward itself but rather in the way it is dispensed. So, how can we make rewards motivational? Some commonly mentioned tips:

- Do not overuse rewards.
- Do not take the rewards terribly seriously (e.g. I have always used sweets or cookies very successfully with university students or adult learners who appreciated them but also considered them a laugh).
- Make sure that the reward has some kind of lasting visual representation as well (such as a certificate or a badge accompanying a non-material reward) so that students have something in hand to take home and to show people.
- Make rewards meaningful to the students. One good way of ensuring this is letting the students themselves choose the reward.
- Offer rewards as unexpected gifts to show your appreciation after students have already completed the task.
- Offer rewards for complex activities which require prolonged engagement and creativity on the students' part.
- Offer rewards for trying out activities that the students have had no experience with so that they can get a taste for them.
- Offer rewards for engaging in activities that offer consistent, incremental success to the participants (so that they can be 'hooked').

Strategy 34

Offer rewards in a motivational manner.

More specifically:

- Make sure that students do not get too preoccupied with the rewards.
- Make sure that even non-material rewards have some kind of lasting visual representation.
- Offer rewards for participating in activities that students may get drawn into because they require creative goal-oriented behaviour and offer novel experiences and consistent success.

Grades

For motivational psychologists 'grade' is definitely a 'four-letter word'. Grades are seen as the ultimate 'baddies', representing everything that is wrong with contemporary education, with its emphasis on the product rather than on the process, and with its preoccupation with comparing, rank ordering and pigeon-holing students rather than accepting them on their individual merits. Because of their ultimate importance in every facet of the education system, grades frequently become equated in the minds of school children with a sense of self-worth; that is, they consider themselves only as worthy as their school-related achievements, regardless of their personal characteristics such as being loving, good or courageous (Covington and Teel 1996). Assessment is the area where achievement-based societies and student-centred teaching principles inevitably clash.

Regrettably . . .

'Schools are expected to function both to teach students and to segregate them, that is, in this latter instance, to identify those youngsters who are likely to profit the most from further instruction. This function is part of the larger sorting process by which all individuals are eventually allocated proportionately to the available jobs across society, some of which (the fewest number) are the most prestigious or lucrative. The nurturing of talent and the selection of talent are essentially incompatible goals, and teachers are caught in between.'
(Martin Covington and Karen Manheim Teel 1996:37)

Let us look at the main concerns about grades and grading that are often mentioned by teachers and researchers (cf. Brophy 1998 and Covington and Teel 1996):

- Getting good grades can become more important than learning; in other words, grades tend to focus students' attention on concerns about meeting demands successfully rather than on any personal benefits that they might derive from the learning experience.
- Grades may put students and teachers into two opposite camps and often make it difficult for teachers to follow modern, student-centred principles.
- Grades may encourage cheating or uncritical student compliance, since learners may be under extreme pressure to live up to the set standards. Furthermore, grades often reflect the teacher's perception

of a student's compliance or good behaviour rather than academic merit.

- Grades are often highly subjective and sometimes are not applied for the right reasons. For example, in the field of language education, test scores rarely reflect the level of communicative competence, since there is a lack of standardised assessment techniques to measure several crucial areas of this competence (e.g. pragmatic knowledge or strategic competence).
- Grades tend to aggravate social inequality as the strong get stronger and the weak get weaker.
- Grades tend to focus students' attention on ability rather than effort.
- The knowledge of being assessed increases student anxiety.

Regrettably . . .

'Certainly, many students are grade driven, not to say, 'grade grubbing', and this preoccupation begins surprisingly early in life.' (Martin Covington 1999:127)

Having done some rather satisfying grade-bashing, let us now come back to earth and see what we can do about eliminating some of the bad motivational effects of grades. After all, at least for the foreseeable future, grades are likely to remain a fact of life. Parents expect them, education authorities require them, college admission tutors rely on them and, in general, society uses them to distribute its job resources and career paths among the multiple applicants. As Covington and Teel (1996:43) conclude, 'Teachers cannot be expected to defy such entrenched traditions. Grades and grading are here to stay.'

Because grading has been such a concern for most educationalists, we should not be surprised that the list of possible remedies is extensive. However, we are also likely to find that only a few of the suggestions are specifically relevant to or applicable in our special instructional circumstances. Anyway, here is a menu of strategies to choose from:

- The rating system should be absolutely *transparent*, that is, it should be obvious right from the start what the success criteria are. You could provide students with models to illustrate what constitutes exemplary performance. Alternatively, or in addition to this, you could have students practise using the list of assessment criteria to evaluate themselves on an assignment.
- When marking written assignments, complement grades with comments that deliver praise and suggestions for improvement. These

notes also provide an ideal opportunity to make personal comments and to offer help.

- Grades should also reflect, as much as possible, the student's *relative improvement* rather than only their standard of achievement as compared to some external criterion. In practical terms this would mean, for example, awarding 'improvement grades' when a student redoes an assignment or makes up for a deficit or redresses an error after receiving corrective feedback. Brophy (1998) stresses that some sort of 'safety net' should always be included in assessment for failing students, for example in the form of opportunities to take an alternative test following a period of reviewing and relearning.

- Involve students in an *ongoing process of evaluation* during the course rather than relying on the results of one or two tests only. The assessment should also cover participation in the lessons or in projects. Alternative measurement tools, such as *portfolio assessment*, might be particularly appropriate for the purpose of continuous assessment. Portfolios are organised sets of student work collected in a folder to illustrate the students' progress over time. A further advantage of portfolio assessment is that learners can exercise a degree of control in deciding what to include in their portfolios, and to revise and improve the items in response to feedback from the teacher or their peers.

- Teacher ratings should be complemented by the students' *self-assessment*; to this effect, provide learners with self-evaluation tools and show that you trust that students can be honest in evaluating their own work (see Table 9 for an example of a self-assessment sheet which was used to determine the students' final grade in a college writing course).

- If appropriate, consider developing a system of *peer grading* (i.e. when students evaluate each other).

- The final rating of a student should be the product of *two-way negotiation*, for example by asking each student's opinion in a personal interview or student conference.

- Rating should be *two-sided*, that is, students should also evaluate the teacher, for example by completing an end-of-term questionnaire.

Wouldn't it be nice . . .?

'Encourage students to see you as allied with them in preparing for tests, not as allied with the test in pressuring or threatening them.'
(Jere Brophy 1998:69)

Table 9 *Sample Self-Assessment Sheet*

Please answer the following questions about yourself by circling the appropriate word or number.

1. I have done a warmer/ice-breaker.	Yes No
2. I have handed in assignments.	All Most Some
3. I have a complete writing file.	Yes No
4. I played an active role in class activities.	5 4 3 2 1
5. I volunteered to be 'scribe' or 'spokesperson' for my pair/group, or 'victim' in the big group.	Several times Twice Once or never
6. My grades for homework, etc. were mostly	5 4 3 2 1
7. How many classes did I miss?	0 1 2 3 4 or more
8. Based on my effort and achievement in Writing this term, I would give myself a	5 4 3 2 1

Thank you!

(Designed by Sarah Thurrell, Eötvös University, Budapest, to determine her student's end-of-term grade in a writing course, using a 1–5 grade system with 5 as the top mark.)

Strategy 35

Use grades in a motivating manner, reducing as much as possible their demotivating impact.

More specifically:

- Make the assessment system completely transparent, and incorporate mechanisms by which the students and their peers can also express their views.
- Make sure that grades also reflect effort and improvement and not just objective levels of achievement.
- Apply continuous assessment that also relies on measurement tools other than pencil-and-paper tests.
- Encourage accurate student self-assessment by providing various self-evaluation tools.

Conclusion: Towards a motivation-sensitive teaching practice

'If you have read through the rest of the book before turning to this chapter, you may be feeling that the whole topic of motivation is much more complicated than you thought. You also may be daunted at the prospect of trying to integrate so many principles into your teaching. This is understandable.'
(Brophy 1998:254)

Having surveyed a wide range of useful motivational strategies and techniques, we must now address the crucial question of what might be the best way of establishing a motivation-sensitive teaching practice. This is an important issue because one thing is fairly certain: for most readers simply starting with Strategy 1 in this book and then systematically going through every one of the long list of strategies is unlikely to be the best option. There is so much to pay attention to in the classroom: language content, teaching methodology, timing, administration, discipline, etc. that for many of us taking on another onerous 'burden' – i.e. to be on a constant 'motivational alert' – may be asking for too much. So what do we do?

The 'good enough motivator'

In an overview of group psychology for educational purposes, Madeline Ehrman and I (1998) have referred to D. W. Winnicott's (1965) concept of the 'good enough mother' as one that we found useful in understanding certain teacher functions. Winnicott's concept has been adopted by many psychologists, and extending it to parenting in general, Bruno Bettelheim (1987) has written a book entitled *A Good Enough Parent*. The concept of the 'good enough parent' suggests that in order to produce psychological health in the child, the parent does *not* need to be perfect. Instead, there is a minimum level of support needed for healthy development, including empathic understanding, soothing, protection and, of course, love. In other words, 'good enough parenting' requires the parent to exceed a certain threshold of quality parenting without necessarily having to be a 'Supermum' or 'Superdad'.

On the 'good enough parent'. . .

'In order to raise the child well one ought not to try to be a perfect parent, as much as one should not expect one's child to be, or to become, a perfect individual. Perfection is not within the grasp of ordinary human beings. Efforts to attain it typically interfere with that lenient response to the imperfections of others, including those of one's child, which alone make good human relations possible.'
(Bruno Bettelheim 1987:ix)

Following the *'good enough'* analogy, it is my belief that teachers should aim to become 'good enough motivators' rather than striving unreasonably to achieve 'Supermotivator' status. When you look at all the ideas presented in this book, don't think for a moment that you have to apply all of them to do a decent job. I do not think anyone could do that – personally, I have consistently applied only a fraction of the long list of strategies discussed earlier. What we need is *quality* rather than quantity. A few well-chosen strategies that suit both you and your learners might take you beyond the threshold of the 'good enough motivator', creating an overall positive motivational climate in the classroom. Some of the most motivating teachers often rely on a few basic techniques!

A stepwise approach

Yes!

'It will take time to implement the strategies suggested in this book. Try a few things with a few students. See what happens. If you find the strategies helpful, you will find a way to use them more and more. Your success can then be a model for your colleagues.'
(Barbara McCombs and James Pope 1994:118)

What I suggest is a stepwise approach. In the tables below, I have listed all the boxed strategies from the previous chapters. Using these lists, you can take the following steps:

> As a first step, go through the lists and identify those motivational strategies that are already part of your teaching practice – put a tick in the relevant boxes in the *'Part of my teaching'* column.
> Take an area that you have marked and by looking up the relevant sections in the book reinforce this motivational practice in your classes by making it more systematic and varied.
> Alternatively, you may want to address a strategic area that has not been part of your past teaching practice but which you feel might work with you and your students. Select one or two (but not more) specific techniques that you will try out in a class. Once you have given them a try, put a tick in the *'Tried it out'* column. If the strategies work – that is, if you feel comfortable with them and the students are sufficiently responsive – keep applying the strategies in your other classes as well until you have automated them enough to be able to tick off the *'Part of my teaching'* column.
> After a while you may be ready to experiment with another strategy, addressing another motivational area. However, let us not forget that the 'good enough motivator' takes it easy. And, as Covington and Teel (1996:98) state, 'Fortunately, even small changes initiated early on can make substantial changes down the line in terms of student motivation and achievement, as well as teacher morale.'

Good luck and lots of ticks!

MOTIVATIONAL STRATEGIES: CREATING THE BASIC MOTIVATIONAL CONDITIONS	Tried it out	Part of my teaching
1 Demonstrate and talk about your own enthusiasm for the course material, and how it affects you personally.		
Share your own personal interest in the L2 with your students.		
Show students that you value L2 learning as a meaningful experience that produces satisfaction and enriches your life.		
2 Take the students' learning very seriously.		
Show students that you care about their progress.		
Indicate your mental and physical availability for all things academic.		
Have sufficiently high expectations for what your students can achieve.		

MOTIVATIONAL STRATEGIES: CREATING THE BASIC MOTIVATIONAL CONDITIONS	Tried it out	Part of my teaching
3 Develop a personal relationship with your students.		
Show students that you accept and care about them.		
Pay attention and listen to each of them.		
Indicate your mental and physical availability.		
4 Develop a collaborative relationship with the students' parents.		
Keep parents regularly informed about their children's progress.		
Ask for their assistance in performing certain supportive tasks at home.		
5 Create a pleasant and supportive atmosphere in the classroom.		
Establish a norm of tolerance.		
Encourage risk-taking and have mistakes accepted as a natural part of learning.		
Bring in and encourage humour.		
Encourage learners to personalise the classroom environment according to their taste.		
6 Promote the development of group cohesiveness.		
Try and promote interaction, cooperation and the sharing of genuine personal information among the learners.		
Use ice-breakers at the beginning of a course.		
Regularly use small-group tasks where students can mix.		
Encourage and if possible organise extracurricular activities and outings.		
Try and prevent the emergence of rigid seating patterns.		
Include activities that lead to the successful completion of whole-group tasks or involve small-group competition games.		
Promote the building of a group legend.		
7 Formulate group norms explicitly, and have them discussed and accepted by the learners.		
Include a specific 'group rules' activity at the beginning of a group's life to establish the norms explicitly.		
Explain the importance of the norms you mandate and how they enhance learning, and ask for the students' agreement.		

MOTIVATIONAL STRATEGIES: CREATING THE BASIC MOTIVATIONAL CONDITIONS	Tried it out	Part of my teaching
Elicit suggestions for additional rules from the learners and discuss these in the same way as the rules you have proposed.		
Put the group rules (and the consequences for violating them) on display.		
8 Have the group norms consistently observed.		
Make sure that you yourself observe the established norms consistently.		
Never let any violations go unnoticed.		

MOTIVATIONAL STRATEGIES: GENERATING INITIAL MOTIVATION	Tried it out	Part of my teaching
9 Promote the learners' language-related values by presenting peer role models.		
Invite senior students to talk to your class about their positive experiences.		
Feedback to the students the views of their peers, e.g. in the form of a class newsletter.		
Associate your learners with peers (e.g. in group or project work) who are enthusiastic about the subject.		
10 Raise the learners' intrinsic interest in the L2 learning process.		
Highlight and demonstrate aspects of L2 learning that your students are likely to enjoy.		
Make the first encounters with the L2 a positive experience.		
11 Promote 'integrative' values by encouraging a positive and open-minded disposition towards the L2 and its speakers, and towards foreignness in general.		
Include a sociocultural component in your language curriculum.		
Quote positive views about language learning by influential public figures.		
Encourage learners to conduct their own exploration of the L2 community (e.g. on the internet).		
Promote contact with L2 speakers and L2 cultural products.		

MOTIVATIONAL STRATEGIES: GENERATING INITIAL MOTIVATION	Tried it out	Part of my teaching
12 Promote the students' awareness of the instrumental values associated with the knowledge of an L2.		
Regularly remind students that the successful mastery of the L2 is instrumental to the accomplishment of their valued goals.		
Reiterate the role the L2 plays in the world, highlighting its potential usefulness both for themselves and their community.		
Encourage the learners to apply their L2 proficiency in real-life situations.		
13 Increase the students' expectancy of success in particular tasks and in learning in general.		
Make sure that they receive sufficient preparation and assistance.		
Make sure they know exactly what success in the task involves.		
Make sure that there are no serious obstacles to success.		
14 Increase your students' goal-orientedness by formulating explicit class goals accepted by them.		
Have the students negotiate their individual goals and outline a common purpose, and display the final outcome in public.		
Draw attention from time to time to the class goals and how particular activities help to attain them.		
Keep the class goals achievable by re-negotiating if necessary.		
15 Make the curriculum and the teaching materials relevant to the students.		
Use needs analysis techniques to find out about your students' needs, goals and interests, and then build these into your curriculum as much as possible.		
Relate the subject matter to the everyday experiences and backgrounds of the students.		
Enlist the students in designing and running the course.		
16 Help to create realistic learner beliefs.		
Positively confront the possible erroneous beliefs, expectations, and assumptions that learners may have.		
Raise the learners' general awareness about the different ways languages are learnt and the number of factors that can contribute to success.		

Motivational strategies: Maintaining and protecting motivation	Tried it out	Part of my teaching
17 Make learning more stimulating and enjoyable by breaking the monotony of classroom events.		
Vary the learning tasks and other aspects of your teaching as much as you can.		
Focus on the motivational flow and not just the information flow in your class.		
Occasionally do the unexpected.		
18 Make learning stimulating and enjoyable for the learner by increasing the attractiveness of the tasks.		
Make tasks challenging.		
Make task content attractive by adapting it to the students' natural interests or by including novel, intriguing, exotic, humorous, competitive or fantasy elements.		
Personalise learning tasks.		
Select tasks that yield tangible, finished products.		
19 Make learning stimulating and enjoyable for the learners by enlisting them as active task participants.		
Select tasks which require mental and/or bodily involvement from each participant.		
Create specific roles and personalised assignments for everybody.		
20 Present and administer tasks in a motivating way.		
Explain the purpose and utility of a task.		
Whet the students' appetite about the content of the task.		
Provide appropriate strategies to carry out the task.		
21 Use goal-setting methods in your classroom.		
Encourage learners to select specific, short-term goals for themselves.		
Emphasise goal completion deadlines and offer ongoing feedback.		
22 Use contracting methods with your students to formalise their goal commitment.		
Draw up a detailed written agreement with individual students, or whole groups, that specifies what they will learn and how, and the ways by which you will help and reward them.		

Motivational Strategies in the language classroom

Motivational strategies: Maintaining and protecting motivation	Tried it out	Part of my teaching
Monitor student progress and make sure that the details of the contract are observed by both parties.		
23 Provide learners with regular experiences of success.		
Provide multiple opportunities for success in the language class.		
Adjust the difficulty level of tasks to the students' abilities and counterbalance demanding tasks with manageable ones.		
Design tests that focus on what learners can rather than cannot do, and also include improvement options.		
24 Build your learners' confidence by providing regular encouragement.		
Draw your learners' attention to their strengths and abilities.		
Indicate to your students that you believe in their effort to learn and their capability to complete the tasks.		
25 Help diminish language anxiety by removing or reducing the anxiety-provoking elements in the learning environment.		
Avoid social comparison, even in its subtle forms.		
Promote cooperation instead of competition.		
Help learners accept the fact that they will make mistakes as part of the learning process.		
Make tests and assessment completely 'transparent' and involve students in the negotiation of the final mark.		
26 Build your learners' confidence in their learning abilities by teaching them various learner strategies.		
Teach students learning strategies to facilitate the intake of new material.		
Teach students communication strategies to help them overcome communication difficulties.		
27 Allow learners to maintain a positive social image while engaged in the learning tasks.		
Select activities that contain 'good' roles for the participants.		
Avoid face-threatening acts such as humiliating criticism or putting students in the spotlight unexpectedly.		
28 Increase student motivation by promoting cooperation among the learners.		

MOTIVATIONAL STRATEGIES: MAINTAINING AND PROTECTING MOTIVATION	Tried it out	Part of my teaching
Set up tasks in which teams of learners are asked to work together towards the same goal.		
Take into account team products and not just individual products in your assessment.		
Provide students with some 'social training' to learn how best to work in a team.		
29 *Increase student motivation by actively promoting learner autonomy.*		
Allow learners real choices about as many aspects of the learning process as possible.		
Hand over as much as you can of the various leadership/teaching roles and functions to the learners.		
Adopt the role of a facilitator.		
30 *Increase the students' self-motivating capacity.*		
Raise your students' awareness of the importance of self-motivation.		
Share with each other strategies that you have found useful in the past.		
Encourage students to adopt, develop and apply self-motivating strategies.		

MOTIVATIONAL STRATEGIES: ENCOURAGING POSITIVE SELF-EVALUATION	Tried it out	Part of my teaching
31 *Promote effort attributions in your students.*		
Encourage learners to explain their failures by the lack of effort and appropriate strategies applied rather than by their insufficient ability.		
Refuse to accept ability attributions and emphasise that the curriculum is within the learners' ability range.		
32 *Provide students with positive information feedback.*		
Notice and react to any positive contributions from your students.		

MOTIVATIONAL STRATEGIES: ENCOURAGING POSITIVE SELF-EVALUATION	Tried it out	Part of my teaching
Provide regular feedback about the progress your students are making and about the areas which they should particularly concentrate on.		
33 *Increase learner satisfaction.*		
Monitor student accomplishments and progress, and take time to celebrate any victory.		
Make student progress tangible by encouraging the production of visual records and arranging regular events.		
Regularly include tasks that involve the public display of the students' skills.		
34 *Offer rewards in a motivational manner.*		
Make sure that students do not get too preoccupied with the rewards.		
Make sure that even non-material rewards have some kind of lasting visual representation.		
Offer rewards for participating in activities that students may get drawn into because they require creative goal-oriented behaviour and offer novel experiences and consistent success.		
35 *Use grades in a motivating manner, reducing as much as possible their demotivating impact.*		
Make the assessment system completely transparent, and incorporate mechanisms by which the students and their peers can also express their views.		
Make sure that grades also reflect effort and improvement and not just objective levels of achievement.		
Apply continuous assessment that also relies on measurement tools other than pencil-and-paper tests.		
Encourage accurate student self-assessment by providing various self-evaluation tools.		

Please consider sharing your experiences

The study of motivational strategies is still a largely uncharted territory in L2 education. There is no doubt that student motivation can be consciously increased by using creative techniques, but we know too little about the details of how this could or should happen. Therefore, I would like to ask you to consider sharing some of your own relevant experiences. I would be very much interested to receive accounts of how certain motivational strategies have worked – or have not worked – in your classes. Because real classroom experiences can have an important instructive value, I will, in turn, make efforts to share your accounts with other teachers in various forums, such as in workshops and conference presentations. In order to be able to acknowledge the source of each account, please specify the type of language course it concerns, including the description of the general characteristics of the learner group (e.g. age, mother tongue(s), proficiency level, group size). Whether or not you would like your name to be disclosed is entirely your decision – please let me know if you would like me to disguise or keep confidential some of the details. Thank you very much in anticipation.

Zoltán Dörnyei
zoltan.dornyei@nottingham.ac.uk

References

Ajzen, I. 1988. *Attitudes, Personality and Behavior.* Chicago: Dorsey Press.

Alderman, M. K. 1999. *Motivation for Achievement: Possibilities for Teaching and Learning.* Mahwah, NJ: Lawrence Erlbaum.

Alison, J. 1993. *Not Bothered? Motivating Reluctant Language Learners in Key Stage 4.* London: CILT.

Ames, C. 1992. Classrooms, goals, structures and student motivation. *Journal of Educational Psychology,* 84, 267–271.

Atkinson, J. W. and J. O. Raynor (Eds.) 1974. *Motivation and Achievement.* Washington, DC: Winston and Sons.

Bandura, A. 1997. *Self-Efficacy: The Exercise of Control.* New York: Freeman.

Bandura, A. and D. Schunk 1981. Cultivating competence, self-efficacy and intrinsic interest through proximal self-motivation. *Journal of Personality and Social Psychology,* 41, 586–98.

Baumeister, R. F. 1996. Self-regulation and ego threat: Motivated cognition, self-deception and destructive goal setting. In P. M. Gollwitzer and J. A. Bargh (Eds.) *The Psychology of Action: Linking Cognition and Motivation to Behaviour.* New York: Guilford Press, 27–47.

Benson, P. 2001. *Teaching and Researching Autonomy in Language Learning.* Harlow: Longman.

Berliner, D. C. and R. C. Calfee (Eds.) 1996. *Handbook of Educational Psychology.* New York: Macmillan.

Bettelheim, B. 1987. *A Good Enough Parent.* London: Thames and Hudson.

Brophy, J. E. 1987. Synthesis of research on strategies for motivating students to learn. *Educational Leadership,* 45, 40–48.

Brophy, J. E. 1998. *Motivating Students to Learn.* McGraw-Hill, Boston, MA.

Brophy, J. E. 1999. Toward a model of the value aspects of motivation in education: Developing appreciation for particular learning domains and activities. *Educational Psychologist,* 34, 75–85.

Brophy, J. E. and N. Kher 1986. Teacher socialization as a mechanism for developing student motivation to learn. In R. S. Feldman (Ed.) *The Social Psychology of Education: Current Research and Theory.* Cambridge: Cambridge University Press, 257–288.

Brown, H. D. 1989. *A Practical Guide to Language Learning: A Fifteen-Week Program of Strategies for Success.* Boston, MA: McGraw-Hill.

Brown, H. D. 1994. *Teaching by Principles*. Englewood Cliffs, NJ: Prentice Hall.

Burden, P. R. 1995. *Classroom Management and Discipline*. New York: Longman.

Byram, M. 1997. *Teaching and Assessing Intercultural Communicative Competence*. Clevedon: Multilingual Matters.

Byram, M. 2000. *Routledge Encyclopedia of Language Teaching and Learning*. London: Routledge.

Canfield, J. and H. C. Wells 1994. *100 Ways to Enhance Self-Concept in the Classroom: A Handbook for Teachers, Counselors, and Group Leaders*. Needham Heights, MA: Allyn and Bacon.

Carter, R. and D. Nunan (Eds.) 2001. *Applied Linguistics*. Cambridge: Cambridge University Press.

Chambers, G. N. 1999. *Motivating Language Learners*. Clevedon: Multilingual Matters.

Clément, R. 1980. Ethnicity, contact and communicative competence in a second language. In H. Giles, W. P. Robinson and P. M. Smith (Eds.) *Language: Social Psychological Perspectives*, Oxford: Pergamon, 147–154.

Clément, R, Z. Dörnyei and K. A. Noels 1994. Motivation, self-confidence and group cohesion in the foreign language classroom. *Language Learning*, 44, 417–448.

Cohen, A. D. 1998. *Strategies in Learning and Using a Second Language*. Harlow: Longman.

Cohen, E. 1994. *Designing Groupwork* (2nd ed.). New York: Teachers College Press.

Corno, E. 1993. The best-laid plans: Modern conceptions of volition and educational research. *Educational Researcher*, 22, 14–22.

Corno, L. 1994. Student volition and education: Outcomes, influences, and practices. In D. H. Schunk and B. J. Zimmerman (Eds.) *Self-Regulation of Learning and Performance*. Hillsdale, NJ: Lawrence Erlbaum, 229–251.

Corno, L. and R. Kanfer 1993. The role of volition in learning and performance. *Review of Research in Education*, 19, 301–341.

Corson, D. (Ed.) 1997. *Encyclopedia of Language and Education* (Vols. 1–8). Doerdrecht: Kluwer.

Covington, M. 1992. *Making the Grade: A Self-Worth Perspective on Motivation and School Reform*. Cambridge: Cambridge University Press.

Covington, M. V. 1998. *The Will to Learn: A Guide for Motivating Young People*. Cambridge: Cambridge University Press.

Covington, M. 1999. Caring about learning: The nature and nurturing of subject-matter appreciation. *Educational Psychologist*, 34, 127–136 .

Covington, M. V. and K. M. Teel 1996. *Overcoming Student Failure: Changing Motives and Incentives for Learning*. Washington, DC: American Psychological Association.

Cranmer, D. 1996. *Motivating High Level Learners*. Harlow: Longman.

Crookes, G. and R. W. Schmidt 1991. Motivation: Reopening the research agenda. *Language Learning*, 41, 469–512 .

References

Csikszentmihalyi, M. 1997. Intrinsic motivation and effective teaching: A flow analysis. In J. L. Bess (Ed.) *Teaching Well and Liking It: Motivating Faculty to Teach Effectively.* Baltimore: Johns Hopkins University Press, 72–89.

Dam, L. 1995. *Learner Autonomy 3: From Theory to Practice.* Dublin: Authentik.

Damon, W. and N. Eisenberg (Eds.) 1998. *Handbook of Child Psychology. 5th Edition, Vol. 3: Social, emotional, and personality development.* New York: John Wiley and Sons.

Deci, E. L. and R. M. Ryan 1985. *Intrinsic Motivation and Self-Determination in Human Behavior.* New York: Plenum.

Dembo, M. H. and M. J. Eaton 1997. School learning and motivation. In G. D. Phye (Ed.) *Handbook of Academic Learning: Construction of Knowledge.* San Diego, CA: Academic Press.

Dörnyei, Z. 1994. Motivation and motivating in the foreign language classroom. *Modern Language Journal*, 78, 273–284.

Dörnyei, Z. 1997. Psychological processes in cooperative language learning: Group dynamics and motivation. *Modern Language Journal*, 81, 482–493.

Dörnyei, Z. 2000. Motivation in action: Toward a process-oriented conceptualisation of student motivation. *British Journal of Educational Psychology*, 70, 519–538.

Dörnyei, Z. 2001. *Teaching and Researching Motivation.* Harlow: Longman.

Dörnyei, Z. and K. Csizér 1998. Ten commandments for motivating language learners: Results of an empirical study. *Language Teaching Research*, 2, 203–229.

Dörnyei, Z. and K. Gajdátsy 1989. A student-centred approach to language learning 1. *Practical English Teaching*, 9/3, 43–45.

Dörnyei, Z. and A. Malderez 1997. Group dynamics and foreign language teaching. *System*, 25, 65–81.

Dörnyei, Z. and A. Malderez 1999. Group dynamics in foreign language learning and teaching. In J. Arnold (Ed.) *Affective Language Learning.* Cambridge: Cambridge University Press, 155–169.

Dörnyei, Z. and I. Ottó 1998. Motivation in action: A process model of L2 motivation. *Working Papers in Applied Linguistics* (Thames Valley University, London), 4, 43–69.

Dörnyei, Z. and R. Schmidt (Eds.) 2001. *Motivation and Second Language Acquisition.* Honolulu, HI: University of Hawaii Press.

Dörnyei, Z. and M. L. Scott 1997. Communication strategies in a second language: Definitions and taxonomies. *Language Learning*, 47, 173–210.

Eagly, A. H. and S. Chaiken 1993. *The Psychology of Attitudes.* New York: Harcourt Brace.

Eccles, J. S. and A. Wigfield 1995. In the mind of the actor: The structure of adolescents' achievement task values and expectancy-related beliefs. *Personality and Social Psychology Bulletin*, 21, 215–225.

Ehrman, M. E. and Z. Dörnyei 1998. *Interpersonal Dynamics in Second*

148

Language Education: The Visible and Invisible Classroom. Sage, Thousand Oaks, CA.

Ekbatani, G. and H. Pierson (Eds.) 2000. *Learner-Directed Assessment in ESL.* Mahwah, NJ: Lawrence Erlbaum.

Ford, M. 1992. *Motivating Humans: Goals, Emotions and Personal Agency Beliefs.* Newbury Park, CA: Sage.

Frank, C. and M. Rinvolucri 1991. *Grammar in Action Again: Awareness Activities for Language Learning.* Hemel Hempstead: Prentice Hall.

Galloway, D., C. Rogers, D. Armstrong and E. Leo 1998. *Motivating the Difficult to Teach.* Harlow: Longman.

Garcia, T. and P. R. Pintrich 1994. Regulating motivation and cognition in the classroom: The role of self-schemas and self-regulating strategies. In D. Schunk and B. J. Zimmerman (Eds.) *Self-Regulation of Learning and Performance: Issues of Educational Applications.* Hillsdale, NJ: Lawrence Erlbaum, 127–153.

Gardner, R. C. 1979. Social psychological aspects of second language acquisition. In H. Giles and R. St. Clair (Eds.) *Language and Social Psychology.* Oxford: Blackwell, 193–220.

Gardner, R. C. 1985. *Social Psychology and Second Language Learning: The Role of Attitudes and Motivation.* London: Edward Arnold.

Gardner, R. C. and W. E. Lambert 1972. *Attitudes and Motivation in Second Language Learning.* Rowley, MA: Newbury House.

Gardner, R. C. and P. D. MacIntyre 1993. A student's contributions to second-language learning. Part II: Affective variables. *Language Teaching,* 26, 1–11.

Good, T. L. and J. E. Brophy 1994. *Looking in Classrooms* (6th ed.). New York: HarperCollins.

Graham, S. 1994. Classroom motivation from an attributional perspective. In H. F. O'Neil Jr and M. Drillings (Eds.) *Motivation: Theory and Research.* Hillsdale, NJ: Lawrence Erlbaum, 31–48.

Hadfield, J. 1992. *Classroom Dynamics.* Oxford: Oxford University Press.

Heckhausen, H. 1991. *Motivation and Action.* New York: Springer.

Heckhausen, H. and J. Kuhl 1985. From wishes to action: The dead ends and short cuts on the long way to action. In M. Frese and J. Sabini (Eds.) *Goal-Directed Behaviour: The Concept of Action in Psychology.* Hillsdale, NJ: Lawrence Erlbaum.

Heron, J. 1989. *The Facilitator's Handbook.* London: Kogan Page.

Horwitz, E. K. 1988. The beliefs about language learning of beginning university foreign language students. *Modern Language Journal,* 72, 283–294.

Jones, V. F. and L. S. Jones 1995. *Comprehensive Classroom Management: Creating Positive Learning Environments for All Students* (4th ed.). Needham Heights, MA: Allyn and Bacon.

Juvonen, Y. and K. R. Wentzel (Eds.) 1996. *Social Motivation: Understanding Children's School Adjustment.* New York: Cambridge University Press.

Kaplan, R. (Ed.) In press. *Handbook of Applied Linguistics.* Oxford: Oxford University Press.

References

Keller, J. M. 1983. Motivational design of instruction. In C. M. Reigelruth (Ed.) *Instructional Design Theories and Models: An Overview of their Current Status.* Hillsdale, NJ: Lawrence Erlbaum, 383–434.

Kramsch, C. 1998. *Language and Culture.* Oxford: Oxford University Press.

Kuhl, J. 1987. Action control: The maintenance of motivational states. In F. Halish and J. Kuhl (Eds.) *Motivation, Intention and Volition.* Berlin: Springer, 279–291.

Lightbown, P. M. and N. Spada 1999. *How Languages are Learned* (Revised ed.). Oxford: Oxford University Press.

Little, D. 1991. *Learner Autonomy 1: Definitions, Issues and Problems.* Dublin: Authentik.

Locke, E. A. and G. P. Latham 1990. *A Theory of Goal Setting and Task Performance.* Englewood Cliffs, NJ: Prentice Hall.

Lustig, M. W. and J. Koester 1999. *Intercultural Competence: Interpersonal Communication Across Cultures.* New York: Longman.

Maslow, A. H. 1970. *Motivation and Personality* (2nd ed.). New York: Harper and Row.

MacIntyre, P. D. 1999. Language anxiety: A review of the research for language teachers. In D. J. Young (Ed.) *Affect in Foreign Language and Second Language Learning.* Boston, MA: McGraw-Hill, 24–45.

McCombs, B. L. and J. E. Pope 1994. *Motivating Hard to Reach Students.* Washington, DC: American Psychological Association.

McCombs, B. L. and J. S. Whisler 1997. *The Learner-Centered Classroom and School: Strategies for Increasing Student Motivation and Achievement.* San Francisco, CA: Jossey-Bass.

Murphey, T. 1998a. Motivating with near peer role models. In B. Visgatis (Ed.) *On JALT'97: Trends and Transitions.* Tokyo: JALT, 205–209.

Murphey, T. 1998b. *Language Hungry: An Introduction to Language Learning Fun and Self-Esteem.* Tokyo: Macmillan Languagehouse.

Noels, K. A., R. Clément and L. G. Pelletier 1999. Perceptions of teachers' communicative style and students' intrinsic and extrinsic motivation. *Modern Language Journal,* 83, 23–34.

Nyikos, M. and R. Oxford (Eds.) 1997. Interaction, collaboration, and cooperation: Learning languages and preparing language teachers. Special Issue. *Modern Language Journal,* 81/4.

O'Malley, J. M. and A. U. Chamot 1990. *Learning Strategies in Second Language Acquisition.* New York: Cambridge University Press.

Oxford, R. L. 1990. *Language Learning Strategies: What Every Teacher Should Know.* Boston, MA: Heinle and Heinle.

Oxford, R. L. and M. Nyikos 1997. Interaction, collaboration, and Cooperation: Learning Languages and Preparing Language Teachers. Special Issue. *Modern Language Journal,* 81/4.

Oxford, R. L. and J. Shearin 1994. Language learning motivation: Expanding the theoretical framework. *Modern Language Journal,* 78, 12–28.

Passe, J. 1996. *When Students Choose Content: A Guide to Increasing Motivation, Autonomy, and Achievement.* Thousand Oaks, CA: Corwin Press.

Pintrich, P. R. and D. H. Schunk 1996. *Motivation in Education: Theory, Research and Applications*. Englewood Cliffs, NJ: Prentice Hall.

Raffini, J. P. 1993. *Winners without Losers: Structures and Strategies for Increasing Student Motivation to Learn*. Needham Heights, MA: Allyn and Bacon.

Raffini, J. P. 1996. *150 Ways to Increase Intrinsic Motivation in the Classroom*. Needham Heights, MA: Allyn and Bacon.

Roberts, C. M. Byram, A. Barro, S. Jordan and B. Street 2001. *Language Learners as Ethnographers*. Clevedon: Multilingual Matters.

Rogers, C. R. and H. J. Freiberg 1994. *Freedom to Learn*. Englewood Cliffs, NJ: Prentice Hall.

Rosenthal, R. and L. Jacobson 1968. *Pygmalion in the Classroom*. New York: Holt, Rinehart and Winston.

Scheidecker, D. and W. Freeman 1999. *Bringing out the Best in Students: How Legendary Teachers Motivate Kids*. Thousand Oaks, CA: Corwin Press.

Schmitt, N. (Ed.) In press. *An Introduction to Applied Linguistics*. London: Arnold.

Schneider, B., M. Csikszentmihalyi, and S. Knauth 1995. Academic challenge, motivation and self-esteem: The daily experience of students in high school. In M. T. Hallinan (Ed.) *Restructuring Schools: Promising Practices and Policies*. New York: Plenum, 175–195.

Seelye, H. N. 1993. *Teaching Culture: Strategies for Intercultural Communication*. Lincolnwood, IL: National Textbook Company.

Senior, R. 1997. Transforming language classes into bonded groups. *ELT Journal*, 51, 3–11.

Silva, D. P. S. 2001. Motivational factors: A case study. Unpublished seminar paper. School of English Studies, University of Nottingham.

Sinclair, B. 1999. More than an act of faith? Evaluating learner autonomy. In C. Kennedy (Ed.) *Innovation and Best Practice in British ELT*. Harlow: Longman, 96–107.

Slavin, R. E. 1996. Research on cooperative learning and achievement: What we know, what we need to know. *Contemporary Educational Psychology*, 21, 43–69.

Snow, R. E., L. Corno and D. N. Jackson 1996. Individual differences in affective and conative functions. In D. C. Berliner and R. C. Calfee (Eds.) *Handbook of Educational Psychology*. New York: Macmillan, 243–310.

Spolsky, B. (Ed.) 1999. *Concise Encyclopedia of Educational Linguistics*. Oxford: Elsevier.

Stipek, D. J. 1996. Motivation and instruction. In D. C. Berliner and R. C. Calfee (Eds.) *Handbook of Educational Psychology*. New York: Macmillan, 85–113.

Tomalin, B. and S. Stempleski 1993. *Cultural Awareness*. Oxford: Oxford University Press.

Underhill, A. 1999. Facilitation in language teaching. In J. Arnold (Ed.) *Affective Language Learning*. Cambridge: Cambridge University Press, 125–141.

References

Ushioda, E. 1996. *Learner Autonomy 5: The Role of Motivation*. Dublin: Authentik.

Ushioda, E. 1997. The role of motivational thinking in autonomous language learning. In D. Little and B. Voss (Eds.) *Language Centres: Planning for the New Millennium*. Plymouth: CERCLES, Centre for Modern Languages, University of Plymouth, 39–50.

Vallerand, R. J. 1997. Toward a hierarchical model of intrinsic and extrinsic motivation. *Advances in Experimental Social Psychology*, 29, 271–360.

Weiner, B. 1984. Principles for a theory of student motivation and their application within an attributional framework. In R. Ames and C. Ames (Eds.) *Research on Motivation in Education: Student Motivation* (Vol. 1). San Diego, CA: Academic Press, 15–38.

Weiner, B. 1992. *Human Motivation: Metaphors, Theories and Research*. Newbury Park, CA: Sage.

Weiner, B. 1994. Integrating social and personal theories of achievement motivation. *Review of Educational Research*, 64, 557–573.

Wentzel, K. R. 1999. Social-motivational processes and interpersonal relationships: Implications for understanding motivation at school. *Journal of Educational Psychology*, 91, 76–97.

Williams, M. 1994. Motivation in foreign and second language learning: An interactive perspective. *Educational and Child Psychology*, 11, 77–84.

Williams, M. and R. Burden 1997. *Psychology for Language Teachers*. Cambridge: Cambridge University Press.

Winnicott, D. W. 1965. *The Maturational Process and the Facilitating Environment*. London: Hogarth Press.

Wlodkowski, R. J. 1986. *Enhancing Adult Motivation to Learn*. San Francisco, CA: Jossey-Bass.

Wong, M. M. and M. Csikszentmihalyi 1991. Motivation and academic achievement: The effects of personality traits and the quality of experience. *Journal of Personality*, 59, 539–574.

Young, D. J. (Ed.) 1999. *Affect in Foreign Language and Second Language Learning*. Boston, MA: McGraw-Hill.

Index

Index